AF440581

"Love Poems and verses without a soul."
By Juan D. Jiménez.
Pseudonym: Luan Vidad.

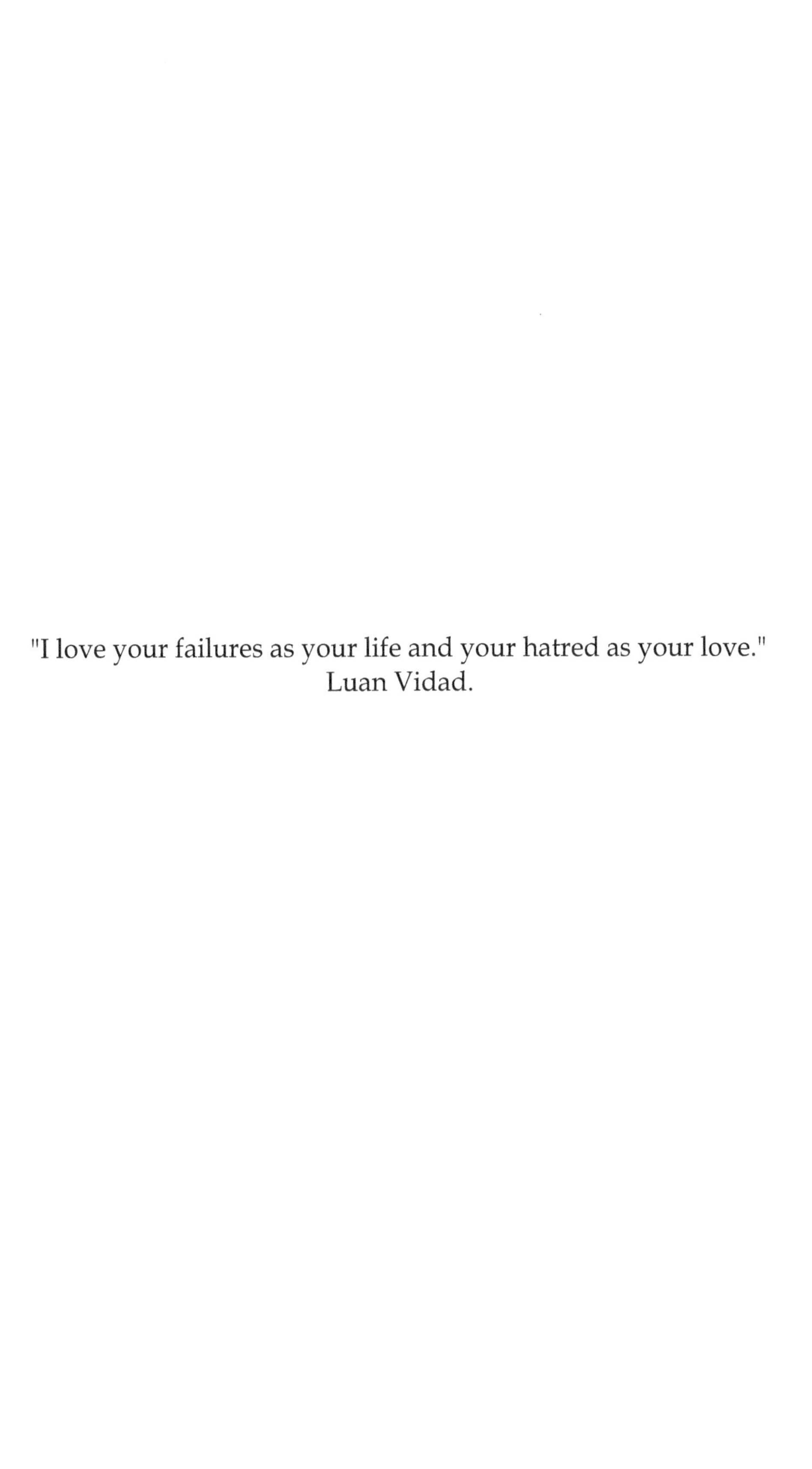

"I love your failures as your life and your hatred as your love."
Luan Vidad.

Author's note.

The work of my fingers and the creativity of my intellect will write the best prologue that my neurons will praise, after assembling the puzzle of another of my forgotten manuscripts and that I corrected at random, -why not? - before publishing them, pseudonym of creativity and feeling in the best state of mind: "Veni, Vidi, Vici:" yes, because in one way or another that is what is the breadth of poetry is all about, the caliber of a good poet, when he manages to write hundreds of poems and thousands of verses.
"Poems of love and verses without a soul" is a simple book or not, sterile or fertile, that perhaps will make you think, doubt, and not believe. What do I know...! It arose from forgotten notes, literature to recycle and that some poets with time, keep in digital files, on paper and that they look at with doubt, skepticism, indifference, and creativity, trying to build among a sea of letters, the riddle where it hides the past, the present and perhaps the future of what they call literature: frustration, hatred, love, nihilism, etc., questioning the rain, not its abundance, the clouds for their color, the spots of the sun and not their greatness, the poverty and not those who fertilize it in the people, social inequalities and not the umbilical cord of the mafias of so many corrupt governments, parasites and of so many socialist dictatorships, which in Latin America, multiply and call themselves a democracy.
And without knowing the reason for the lyricism, the poet threshes the verses in the forge of his mind and at a loop of emotions, feelings, and identity, mother of all the arts, without trying to imitate those mediocre bards, who by no means and having their own voice, filled with a colorless intimacy, distinguish the sublimity of the horizon and not the hell that makes the extraordinary of the horizon possible.

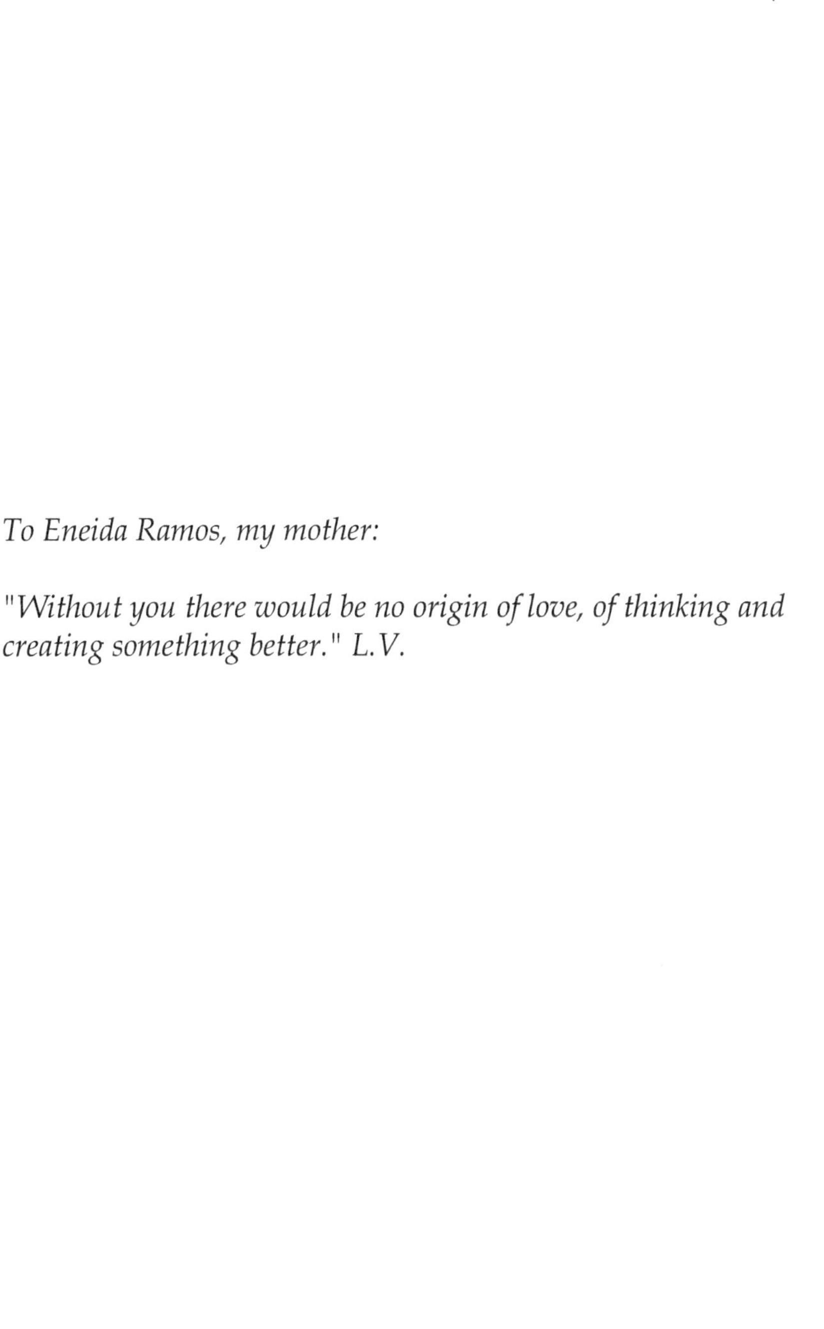

To Eneida Ramos, my mother:

"Without you there would be no origin of love, of thinking and creating something better." L.V.

At any dawn woman,
you shake my manhood
like steel melting in the forge
and what I wear on my chest,
deep in the flesh,
will not end sooner
nor after loving you,
even if it consumes
at the stake of passion
the fire of those who love each other.

And everything for you is spring
with the burst of colors
of the emotions that flood
what touches the tide of love,
when you give it all up
with or without the consent of the heart.

I pretend to forget you.

I pretend to forget you
like summer marginalizes autumn.

I will tear from my memories
those things of yours,
-harmonic and forbidden
deep, simple and sharp, -
that similar to the stabbing
of the past and the present,
-not from the future-
they hurt more inside,
without gushing blood,
but drop by drop,
with the soul shattered
until the end of existence.

__I fish your lips.__

I fish your lips
with the sunset hook
and you lend me your being of bait
without caring about the pain
because you have plenty of love
when you give it all
without caring about anything, just love...

And I, with or without you,
landless goblin,
banished silhouette,
I look for you when you are not there
and I stay up late with the complicity
of the dark to undress you
with what is left over to the imagination,
between each syllable of a banned verse,
broken with happiness, with fright,
between your sex and mine.

Melancholia.

Once again the year
slipped away from us,
shrinking everything,
like the monotony
of the winter air
in the loop of nature.

And yesterday we fled forever
without forgetting to forge poetry
in the arena of life
and I wrote for you,
-among those who dream and do not sleep,-
more than a love poem.

At our age.

At our age
love blossoms inside,
takes root on the outside,
it has no seeds,
it is a spring that seeps
discreetly in the earth
nourished by minerals
and the extract of nature.

At our age
bitter wines no longer exist,
neither good nor bad friends,
God is no longer all-powerful
and the devil is no longer an enemy;
sadness is joy and pain happiness,
the dawns have renounced the sunset
and in the grooves of the aged faces
there remain the indelible traces of the years
as the mournful witnesses of the present.

Of eternities. -X-

Lost in the resonances of the past
I look for the hubbub of your love
and not the indifference of pride,
so that your being and mine
versify your delicate and soft beauty
and in the wailing of the dark,
-naked both of us, -
we ride the steed of passion
and in the attempt to love,
we thresh happiness, poverty and wealth,
and thanks to our bodies
they steal from space what we feel,
before and after that concludes
darkness and light.

With the affability
of your eyes
I sing to your beauty
and with sensuality
of your curves
asymmetrical and bold,
love fuses
the taste of living
and spill the liquor
of my blood
in your lips,
sketching your divinity
on the horizon of your face,
woman.

Love.

Love, do not go,
long are the hours
and intricate the labyrinths
of pleasure;
stay with me tonight,
-it doesn't matter, just tonight-
because passion
cut the veins
with the daggers of love
and I'm scared
for what I feel for you,
fear of losing you
at any moment
to empty this feeling
like a pitcher that breaks
in the wasteland of everything
of nothing, without you.

By you...

I love you because you are my other half,
without form, without luster,
without truth, without lies,
original, almost perfect,
decadent and prosperous, bordering on the sublime.

I love you because you are a woman,
beauty in the pupil,
miniature in the vast,
micro world, latitude,
candor in the essence of the best fragrance,
rhymes that inspire kisses,
the peace that dilates the ephemeral
of loving, of thinking,
to endure and long without chains.

And every part of you, immortal,
it is not measured by love or hate,
passion does not taste it
because it spreads on the skin
of those who love and do not fit
in the universe of life.

I will be discreet.

I will be discreet
like the air lulling the grass,
to the black tulips,
to the olive trees in calm,
to the premature dew of the dawn,
to the lament of the sunset tearing
in the landscape, in the distance.

I will be discreet like the streams
sneaking into the ground
with the consent of nature
and with this elusive poem
like impossible loves,
that do not fuse and coincide,
one day I did not wonder what she felt
when I looked into her eyes
and we let everything pass
and without realizing why,
empty questions remained
hung in the years and we couldn't go back
the time to try, -maybe- again.

More than four strings.

More than four strings hang
on the lintel of oblivion,
one is attached to my weak neck,
for loving freedom,
the lyricism of art and not fictional justice
of my country in ruins,
of my people enslaved for more than half a century
for the Castro dictatorship.

And always the same:
a headless lion, an eagle without wings,
a dried carrot,
a toilet with cobwebs,
and those mouths without teeth,
third world metaphor.

And no one will change your dream
-not mine,-
for a surreal chimera,
although amnesty international
managed to elucidate the pain
of millions of political prisoners
condemned on our prison island,
as the worst passive extermination camp
that exists in Latin America.

Here the stones cry
on the rubble of desolation;
the trees innovate quiet melodies
with the extravagance of the winds
and on the cold marble tombstones,
in this no man's land, -of all, -
defiant crosses rise
in tombs and niches:
symbol of faith, love, and hope
that one day they harvested their hands,
the legs, the feet,
before leaving for the origin
from the ashes, from space, from eternity
and here where the past and the present
they dress in skeletons, in corpses,
of waste and compost,
everything fits in empty basins,
in the most fictitious forgiveness,
in the mythical resurrection,
in love, in the absence and hatred
turned into a religion.

Where will they go...?

Where will they go
the black waters and crystal clear waters
when they mix
like love and hate,
like life and death,
like good and evil ...?
Where will they go ...?

Who will know better than you:
land, serene, rain, sea,
meat, feeling ..?

Where will the dirty waters go
and the crystal clear waters
in the relief of the planet
sharp as a razor,
willing to cut it all
to destroy everything, to transform everything
in powder, in ashes, in gases,
in the matter in space
that they will not occupy our bodies again,
like black water
and clean waters when mixed.

Only.

Alone,
I shipwrecked in you
where your caresses are like the waves
in the Caribbean Sea.

And I swim in your being,
contemplating in your face
the imitation of a paradise
real and not absurd
and without reaching your depth,
that makes me float, that drags me
in the hangover of your thighs,
of your legs and leads me
into your sex where it hides
among honeysuckle
like the flower of life,
there art and inspiration is born,
continuity:
metaphor, lyricism, beginning, and end.

I love your beauty.

I love your beauty,
the contours that limit your curves,
the scale of your shoulders,
what blooms above your epidermis.

I love the intrigue of my fingers
creating love poems
and verses without a soul
in the lines of your lips
that they draw with the brushes
of the art of living, the forbidden:
love, passion,
the concave, the convex,
the sensitivity of being, of not being,
without caring about hiding from the light
to conquer us without fear of the night.

I slip slowly.

I slip through your tributaries,
wet with desire.

And our mouths tune
music of two
with the notes that spring from the heart
when you love without asking permission
and the caresses spread
as it lengthens in the universe.

And it is not easy to go up and down,
go in and out, take off your clothes
at any time to touch you
pretending we're naked
surrounded by so much loneliness
and dressed in fear of existing.

Your estrangement
jump the walls of oppression,
the fences of melancholy,
lifting the stairs
of happiness with the steps
of sadness and joy,
-tumult of uncertainty-
and escapes like a shadow
towards exile,
-involuntary ostracism-
where all that withers
it is a vestige of autumn,
synonymous with exodus,
of the unfathomable ocean,
of current without tide,
without direction...

Of nostalgia.

I think of you,
of tightrope and trampoline
dispelling this nostalgia
that trembles my nerves
and I try to forget you
with the sensuality
from a bottle of liquor
after loving you so much
and have lost you forever…

Like a spectrum.

Like a specter
passerby in the silence,
I look for the saltpeter in the sea
and from the blue of the sky,
the immensity
and the verses bleed
of the confined poet
and their memories explode
like a moon lover Lorca,
of a green that I want you green,
and I sketch in my universe,
the love that I have no excess,
the hate that I find difficult to distribute
and I plowed in the water
and I sowed in the desert white roses…

Lend me your other eye.

Lend me your other eye
half of your brain,
some of your fingers
sharp and nail-less
to write a different poem
to pain, to sadness,
to the mimicry of happiness
blowing up balloons at fictitious Christmas
of those who dream of living in the West,
far from third worlds,
of an unequal and hungry Africa,
of a Latin America with so many corrupt governments
and too many socialist dictatorships.

Will I have to thresh
the verses in the loop of injustice,
without daring to slice my tongue
in a song that is not yours, yes mine,
for being my song made of silence,
of the fear and indifference of the peoples.

Fragments.

"To Miguel Hernández."

1

*There are hearts
that they are lone wolves
in the steppe of desire,
and they are on the prowl looking
victims to bury them
without mercy
the fangs of love and hate.*

2

*It will hurt me not to see you,
your departure will be my escape
and have loved you too much
was living in hell
thinking that I have lost you
without looking for the feeling
an explanation.*

3

*Far away in a strange country
a child cries, because of the war
they murdered his childhood,
they killed their parents
and also their brothers.
They left that child abandoned,
without water,
without bread and without anything,
with his home destroyed*

how they destroyed his city,
and his innocence
in the shortness of his life.

4

What are we in the dark
when we are asleep,
full on the inside, empty on the outside?
What are we during the day when we are
awake and forget to dream
without caring about anything?

5

Of the two stones in your eyes
and mine we build the roads
where the horizon doesn't end
in a faraway country.

6

The seas dried up,
the clouds disappeared,
the atmosphere faded
and humanity disappears
as the last endangered species.

7

I think I haven't changed
though another wrinkle runs through
the continent of my being
and my skin like the tents of a circus

report half of the middle
century of my bones.

8

Love like good wine
it ends, you have to harvest it,
that grows, matures and ferments
to turn it into the liquor of life.

9

My hands flutter without heaven,
they are not steeds and they ride
in fantasy, searching
your love and not desire…

10

I love you because we talk
in the language of silence
and you don't lie when you prolong
sadness and you reduce joy,
because you are the butterfly
that perches on the tree of my body
and flutters in my heart.

11

I wish you like the air
when we slip away
with the privacy of the two,
multiplying those things
that we feel with the complicity of love.

12

With our separation
I will tie my shoes
I will go without luggage,
I will look for the landscapes
in the memories,
tired of living
but never to love you again.

13

The verse does not grow old,
in perpetual youth
does not know about souls,
of gods, or demons,
neither love nor hate
and in her pure innocence
it is a white rose.

14

Mine, waterfall that wets
the stones of loneliness.
Mine, darkness of the universe,
breeze that plays with the waves
on the shores of a beach.

15

We turn without explanation
we go round and round.
Twists of death,
twists of life,

twists in gravity;
we roll in a sphere,
that like a grain of sand
spins and spins in space
without knowing until when, nor why.

16

As you loved me there will be no other, impossible.
They may imitate your kisses
your flattery defoliating in the autumn of desire,
the freshness of your skin, canvas in the brushstrokes
of my fingers, unfinished work ...

17

They divide us with borders,
with languages, with cultures,
with gods and demons,
with tyrannical, manipulative prophets,
with laws and governments,
in the name of democracy,
of socialism and capitalism,
with the art of manipulation,
of wars, of conflicts,
of injustice, of poverty,
of the rich and the poor.

18

Did you know...?
They say that everything costs work,
sacrifice, sweat and tears

in the market of life,
but not love and hate.

19

Leave, set sail, never return,
leave the past in the present
and the future reaping iniquities,
in a foreign country,
on the paths of exile
that divides the dead from the living.

20

Life again.
Who will feast on trouble and tribulation,
misery in third worlds
where to survive on an empty stomach
and with the terror of injustice,
it is the daily reality of many peoples.

21

After wandering
through the cemeteries,
through the cities of the living,
I need you more
because your memory,
a mix of everything and nothing,
pierce the my neurons.

22

Sometimes you sprout

wet and without clothes,
without leaning on the nails
of the mythical Jesus of the Nazarene.

23

You cheat on me
and I believe you,
I'd rather see you lie
and not lose you
because of the truth.

24

My hope was green
like the grass in the meadow
and one day it was eaten
by the goats of the imagination.

25

Melancholy yours,
bleeding slowly
and in the sullen sunset
losing the virginity.

26

They all hurt one extra zero
an one less, because we are poor,
rich, greedy, altruistic,
because we invented
love and hate, the war and the peace,
god and the devil,

27

feeling more beastly
or less human.

27

I discovered you in poetry,
I rhymed you in my paws,
I believed in art because of your perfection
and in love for your sensuality.

28

When it snows
in this desert
the stones sing,
break the mourning of the dust,
they dress up in white,
and they get married.

29

I do not want to see you,
your love hurts me
when I need it most
throwing me mercilessly
the missiles of indifference.

30

Soldier if you are not a pawn,
you are a mercenary, a traitor
at the service of any tyrant,
accomplice of injustice,
who lends himself to kill

innocents in conflicts
and in wars invented by men.

31

They hide the truth from us
and they deceive us with falsehood.
We know nothing of our origin,
of the origin of nothing, of the origin of everything.

32

When flowers languish
the most perfect beauty
in our world,
dies inside and out.

33

My Alfredillo will be forever
that naughty and innocent boy
that I knew before he was born
in his mother's womb.

34

I'm afraid to measure the feeling
because your love surpasses
the limits of infinity.

35

I will die, not of love or sadness,
I'll die savoring poverty

and abhorring
to the corrupt who are handed out
the crumbs of our world.

36

You say my verse
it has no wings, it flies
in the universe of melancholy,
of suffering and in his calvary.
Don't you know what it's about
made mankind?

37

There are lips that do not kiss
that float and sink
in the sea of skin
and they pretend to love.

38

I denounce the cruelty of god,
of tyrannical prophets
that control the people
with the fear that it produces,
lies and ignorance.

39

So much of you tastes
like pollen and honey
and all of me
it tastes like hell,

to paradise in the metaphor
of the silent.

40

They play with climate change
with the manipulation of the corona virus,
with the exploitation of nature,
with the pollution, with the holes
in the ozone layer,
with the extermination of the Amazon,
with the destruction of the seas,
of rivers and lakes.
They play lying to people
and they will continue
to annihilate our world,
the capitalists, the democrats,
the socialists, -all! -
until humanity
be the last species in extinction.

41

Nameless verses
euphoric poetry,
everything rhymes in art
of love and hate.

42

Where's Cupid?
I need his poisoned arrows
to lose my mind fot a woman.

43

The city buries you
revives you, it is jail, freedom,
synonymous with injustice
of equality, of poverty,
of hunger and prosperity.

44

I stay in the eye of the fish,
the twists of the hurricane,
in your forbidden mouth,
in the madness of possessing
your feelings.

45

Squeeze the indifference
see you transparent,
wet and knowing
that you are gone.

46

I stopped believing.
Science became my god
and technology in my prophet.
Total, science and technology
they don't manipulate, they don't convert you
in fanatic, in ignorant,
nor a slave to the fear of dying,
damned forever.

47

Everyone is silent, I am not an accomplice
of the propaganda of the socialists
and I watch how they loot
our nations in Latin America
because corruption
in our continent
it is an incurable disease.

48

If you talk about me
do it like my verses:
enemies of you,
friends of love,
lovers of freedom,
fondling fanatics
of a woman.

49

When love ends
What will become of hatred with its poison,
with his elixir without the stomachs
of the good ones, without the hearts
of the wicked?

50

Why the white, the black,
the Indian and the yellow?
Why so many languages and borders
that divide countries

and separate the peoples?
Any god who invented the humanity
with the atrocious experiment
of existence
he is a hideous tyrant!

51

The poet dies, his verses escape,
and rains his clinging poetry
to the bosom of his people.

52

Come Muses! Undress the art!
Give me the immaculate inspiration
whether I am asleep or awake!

53

Tired of living, of dying,
my bones prop up
what's left of me:
laughable ghost, pathetic shadow,
legend of the past, brief account of the present.

54

Children shine like the stars,
-all have their own light, -
they grow like seeds in fertile soil,
rise like trees,
they throw out roots and branches
who sometimes touch the sky.

55

I have a roof to sleep on
shelter from the cold,
from the rain,
of winter and summer,
miniature paradise
that raises its walls
in the underworld of this planet.

56

My Chato is a cheerful pug,
he loves the early morning,
he sleeps during the day and dreams
with colored bones.

57

More than once I forgot to live
I remembered that I am an accident
in the mediocre comedy of life
and love defeated me and not hate.

58

Repeat the same:
bone loop,
blood, tissue;
daily monotony,
captives of uncertainty
of governments,
to believe or be free.

59

I look for your name in the drawers
of privacy and you get lost in the leaves
of the manuscripts
where I keep the memories.

60

I was terribly alone.
And I saw the corpses feasting
in the carnivals of eternity
and life so vulnerable
I saw her building temples
in memory of death.

61

Sentenced in a body, in a skull,
and trapped in the huge cage
of this planet. How ironic!

62

The paper frog comes out of the water,
jump in my house like a pet
without looking for insects to feed.
In the hands of my child, of Dhazin,
the frog is a queen in his origami world.

63

Don't go far from the sea, sailor,
as lovers do not move away

from each other's lips when they embrace
and merge with the delirium
of their bodies!

64

Please me with your being,
endow me with your beauty,
I like the shackles of desire,
the genie of Aladdin's lamp
hidden between your legs.

65

Those echoes ascend
and they descend through your orbits,
where love cuts, hurts, bleeds
and it justifies everything.

66
A sailboat in the distance
brave and light;
the wide and rough sea
with its colossal waves
try to swallow everything
what is on its waters.

67

Your smile creeps,
she promises everything,
design a triumphal arch
in your face.

68

*Don't look for death
in cemeteries,
look for her on foot,
in fictional paradise of humanity.*

69

*There are words that hurt
more than the wounds that do not heal
outside or inside of our bodies.*

70

*The fisherman in his boat
fall in love with the ocean,
and the current drags him
and the sea delivers
the virginity as love
give everything for nothing.*

71

*Gold buys many things,
envelops everything in its purity
and complicates, destroys and kills.*

72

*The waters of Lake Mead
agonize in the Nevada desert
and slowly commit suicide
at the Hoover Damn.*

73

The prison did not hurt you,
nor the injustice of the tyrant
in your shaken Spain
for the war and for the hatred
because your rude and tender verses
they never took flight,
-and if they did-
they saved your art of loving
after you were murdered.

74

Inevitable
is your love, the skein of your voice
untangling kisses,
your hands peeling off what it touches
and the finesse of your charm
defining the sunrise.

75

They get high on the streets
anywhere in the city;
they don't take drugs for love,
to avoid realities, to live without fear,
they get high because there are mafias,
drug dealers, drug cartels,
because the government allows it,
because democracy is not perfect,
for being like this the American dream.

76

Don't look at the moon bitten by resentment,
look for the other half that hasn't eaten it
those who hate and who hang their wickedness
on the coat racks of humanity

77

If I go to pieces,
if I am left in pieces:
What will be the biggest piece
of my body...?

78

The lights of this city
are as unreal as its gleams
and although they adorn the darkness,
his hidden glow
the injustice of his story.

79

To leave, never to return;
the paths of exile
so long they begin
where your name and mine do not exist.

80

I'm not the same as yesterday,
the present is a coffin
that will bury us all.

81

Who won't love you
when I don't stop loving you
not even after I lost you?

82

There is no better melody
that the echo of silence
after leaving…

83

She was a woman
trapped in the body of a man,
-said some.-
He was a prisoner man
in the body of a woman,
-commented others.-
and who will believe it...?

84

My delirium for you made me a poet,
made me a lover of the early morning
and make me enemy of dawn.

85

They did not find the feet of the traveler
and when they spoke to the roads
the stones groaned at his story.

86

Stay for what?
I'd better go away and with the silence
my friends and my enemies
will miss me…

87

A lullaby song
for my new kid:
flapping of birds in the window,
the murmur of the sea and the sky
in the blinds of the heart.

88

The private of two
it tastes like intimacy,
to the mystery, -sublime throbbing, -
to peace after the war,
to sex melting
in the forge of desire.

89

I will not shut up.
When I'm gone, my verses will say
that I was not afraid, -what if I was? -
that I was an anonymous poet
from exile, navigator without oceans,
pilgrim in the desert
of melancholy and oblivion.

90

Galicia will always be with me,
with Margarita and the Tui vineyards:
drizzle in the winter twilight,
cracked summer on the river Miño,
cutting two countries
with his water razor.

91

What do you have in your blood?
Death to the dove, I hate war,
contempt for peace, for the connivance of the poor,
justice without scales?

92

Your love melts me
evaporate my emotions
solidify my manhood,
close my biggest cracks
and conforms to those things
difficult to define
when I'm not with you.

93

Don't look at yourself from the outside
like the landscape at dawn,
discover what you have inside
as the darkness does
without caring about any sun
in the vastness of the universe.

94

I start to take off your clothes,
what is leftover of your anatomy
and without undressing you, I finish
where the explosion begins
of your beauty in my sex.

95

Are your eyelids
the curtains of space,
what opens and closes
the beginning and the end?

96

They took him
to tie a knot
to his tongue and nailed him
on the cross of injustice
of those who write the laws
with little love and a lot of hate.

97

The best tear
slides on the cheek,
leaps out of the eye like dew
without touching the ground.

98

Soldier who learn

*to shoot and they teach you
the trade of war,
do not go to kill,
let the war pass
how injustice happens
dragging death
in the sewers of humanity.*

99

*The sailboat inflates
the sails on the high seas
and like a colt,
sail fast slashing
with her keel to the raging waves
who do not want to be defeated
before kissing the shores
from the lips of the earth.*

100

*Taking care of the enemy
because he wants you
I can't sleep thinking that him
can steal my best love.*

101

*If you cry that the drops
of water that flow
from your eyes,
be sweet tears
and not salty tears.*

102

*We grow old without forgetting
that we were young,
afraid of losing everything
in the race of life
and we accept death
like an unavoidable accident.*

103

*Now that I'm alive
I will denounce the atrocious
life experiment.*

104

*Old like water,
like space,
like dust,
as are our fluids
and our bones.*

105

*Nostalgia chirp,
flutters from branch to branch,
takes away more than a sigh
at sunset in love
of the colors of dawn.*

106

You have to fertilize

*women with what men
don't have at night or at day*

107

*You asked me for an orchid
and I gave you a flower
to perfume you
and her thorns will take care
of your beauty
because that won't do
an orchid with its petals,
no matter how beautiful it is.*

108

*What will I do to make you mine
to discover what you are wearing
premiering like fashion
of those who do not know
how to love?*

109

*Forgive me if I tried everything
if you were ungrateful and difficult,
you killed me so many times
poisoned by your beauty
and you without knowing how to love me.*

110

*Do not believe and doubt,
because to doubt is to be free,*

because to doubt is to live
without imposition and without fear.

111

I fear state terrorism,
to planned injustice
by governments,
to the peoples subjected
for democracy and dictatorships.

112

Let the dead stay
where they are, while the alive people
fight by surviving like beasts.

113

If I gave you love it's because
I learned it from you.
If I never hated
it's because you didn't know
how to hate like I hate
to more than one enemy.

114

Happiness costs
a kidney and half a liver,
and many commit suicide,
-not for being cowards-
without having met her.

115

Without anyone knowing
I bled for freedom,
I curse the dictators
and the controlled peoples
for ignorance and fear
that generates the planned injustice
of governments.

116

Don't mistake poetry
with politics, nor with the art
of manipulation.

117

Tomorrow we won't be the same,
all about failure of existence
will be pulverized by the time
 as it does with the pages of history books.

118

The sea chooses the sailor,
not to the boat that will sail
its waters, nor the sails
that will swell the winds.

119

The poor are poor

the rich are rich,
the sweepers will follow
picking up trash
and the vagabonds drunks
of so much freedom
they take pity on us
because we are the obedient
slaves of monotony
of governments, humanity.

120

My tongue imprisoned in my mouth,
locked between the balusters of my teeth
despise the bars of his prison.

121

With the hands of hate
the oz and the hammer did
bleed the peoples.

122

Hear the rain fall
ringing on the rooftops,
in the ponds, in the fountains,
on the ground and in the streets:
Have you heard a music
more perfect and sublime?

123

Your annoying charm

challenge mobility of nature,
making fun of life
and of death.

124

I am the hand
that does not tie the knot,
the foot that does not limp,
the mouth without teeth
that does not bite,
but it knows how to kiss.

125

The same, again
on the curvature
of the horizon.
Another dawn,
another winter,
another summer,
a drill of clarity
in the perpetual night
and we are not seeds,
we are fruits that ripen,
that rot afterward.

126

I would like to set sail
in your nakedness,
lose myself in your ocean
and in the moons of your eyes

find love without reaching
anchor in a distant port.

127

We dance without clothes
so many times
that we forgot to dress
after loving us
and so we both go out
to the city of lovers.

128

She was so thin
that she penetrated
through my pupils like a needle
digging into the soul.

129

In the capital of the living
many things are honored
and in the suburb of the dead
eternity is always celebrated.

130

How far will we go with wars,
with conflicts, making bombs,
planes, missiles, grenades,
submarines, aircraft carriers,
training armies,

mercenaries, guerrillas,
in the name of socialism,
of bloody revolutions,
of democracy, of capitalism,
digging trenches for the misfortune
of the peoples?

131

My mother left one sunny day in October.
She left like a rose petal
when she rips it off the autumn breeze
in the garden of oblivion.

133

Promise me we'll see each other
on a day without a watch,
that we will embrace being dust
and with the lips of silence
we will love each other forever.

134

Blue and green, white and black,
brown and yellow,
that's how I love you,
that's how I wish you,
as the sky kisses the sea,
and the light penetrates the darkness.

135

Elephant stretches his long nose,

shows that he is the most powerful,
how strong nature is…

136

Those verses of love
that I improvised in her ears
were echoes in the past
remembering that she was mine
in the fleetingness of feeling.

137

The waves beat incessantly
the reefs and the walls
of a Havana boardwalk,
made of happiness and sadness,
of old age and youth,
of hunger and poverty,
of injustice and socialist dictatorship,
of sentiment: mediocrity,
art, music without lyricism,
nightmares and dreams,
hookers, homosexuals:
cream and juice
of the good and the bad,
in a third world country
who stopped in time,
in my Cuba, on my island,
Cinderella of the Caribbean.

138

We are glow, gloom,

ghosts, ghosts,
cave drawings
in the roundness of this planet.

139

If you leave I will love your departure
I will resurrect what we did
because the first love
does not die, it beats in the chest,
and in the grave of the past
I will bury your memories
and I will water with my tears
in the wasteland of ostracism
the flowers that withered
with the incomprehension,
with the vanity,
with envy and pride.

140

My verses have suffered more than me,
dispensing with my fingers,
of the sedition of my neurons,
of resentment that I do not hide in the closet,
of the love that I give when I don't have love.

141

What will I do if I live so long
shaving with the razor of the years
and looking in the mirror of space
my wrinkles, that like channels
cross the panorama of my countenance?

142

*Another day will go this winter
a burning summer will come,
our children will be born and die,
love won't change fashion
and hatred will continue to celebrate victories.*

143

*The moon grows in your belly
and she waits inside you
nine months to be born
the humanity, mother!*

144

*I love it with roots and without soil,
to sow her in the epidermis
and when her fruits ripen
it will taste like honey
on the palate of my soul.*

145

*In the distance a canine barks
in the city of exile
and the monotony
of the early morning
undermine what's left of me:
unfinished affection, insect that stays up late,
broken pockets, my bones propping
the cracked walls of my being.*

145

I say I loved her,
I lost everything for her,
prisoner in the trap of his body.

146

Playing randomly handsome
what I didn't have and I won
pride of a woman.

147

There are blows that annihilate feelings,
that don't heal or leave scars, but if the wounds,
blows that will hurt until the day of death
and that open the flesh with the daggers of hate,
killing us inside slowly
and leaving us alive on the outside.

148

I have a garden in my memories
lizards under the stones
of my memories
and hoop at sea, sew in the rivers
and dew like miraculous pearls
adorn the stems of the flowers,
but not the petals of doom.

149

Open the door love

-don't be afraid-
it's me coming
with the erect mast
and with my candles
inflated with desire
to cross the sea
of your body.

150

I forgot to live
thinking I'd die
and in the attempt to love
I let it all happen.
in the skeleton of time.

151

I will be back
you know it
and you'll go
on the last train
where we met
accidentally.

152

Remember the dead
who are still alive
in the memory of the peoples
and the living who were stillborn
without ever being
remembered by you.

153

Let them go,
let them leave you alone
with the corpse
who smiles happily
In the other room.

154

The mountain at its height
seem discreet the insignificant
and destructive that we are.

155

You don't heal your wounds
you prefer to bleed injustice,
feel the pain of the peoples
without condemning anyone.

156

The girl on my sleepless nights
plays with the waves of the beach,
she makes castles with sand
and she plays imitating
the flight of the seagulls,
in love with the sky
and so much horizon.

157

Mother why your belly died

and you didn't ask for my life
in exchange for yours?

158

They are the ten fingers of my hands
the legs that are left over from my body.

159

I prefer to beg for tenderness,
not the freedom they steal from us
because I am not a slave
of injustice, but of love.

160
My body waits to become a corpse
while I wait to become its empty vault.

161

I saw the witch with her broom
pass through my window,
she didn't fly,
she swept on the street
the garbage of humanity.

162

I will divide the things I never had,
the things I have left will rot
and it's going to be
the best insect party.

163

I wanted to be rich and discovered
that those who have a lot
accumulate the crumbs
who steal from people.

164

Over the years you don't learn to be old,
you understand the lyricism of dying,
at age without notice,
while the boards that hold you
they start to fall slowly.

165

How many like me did you love?
and you went hanging from the clotheslines
winter of indifference?
How many, tell me how many...?

166

Rodolfo was a bad boy
a troubled young man,
drug addict, rebellious, thief,
a teenager, synonymous of everything a little bit,
because of their parents and society.
One day he was wrong about the stone
on the way and dawned on the other side
with a knife that pierced
his heart and a scissors to his belly.

167

you lifted the flight,
I wanted to look for you.
But you went so far
It had no wings
to fly behind you.

168

On the requisitions of the
wrinkles don't hide years,
pain builds up
and the sadness
of what's been experienced.

169

What was life born for?
To burn my body
and turn me into ashes?

170

Woman so much of you
overflows with the amphorae of love
and design the shelves
in the matrix of existence.
171

I cry to you and you at carnivals.
If we're not the same
it's because we're more beasts or less human.

172

They buried him yesterday
and he was so young.
No one saw his countenance in the coffin
because the wings of two white pigeons
covered his consumed face for cancer.

173

When two women talk
they mix happiness
in times of war
and in times of peace.

174

Those who buy your meat
they are the mercenaries of desire,
villains in disguise
of good men.

175

I contemplate myself
in the mirror of your eyes
when in the dark we make love
and I melt in the burning summer
of your blue and white body.

176

Life is an expectation,
monotony, miserable gift

in the short time of living
to die later…

177

I'd like to imitate,
but I have an identity
and I find it hard to be and not be,
don't believe and doubt,
surrounded by enemies,
flatterers and hypocrites.

178

The mother sympathy,
forgiveness and comfort
because his love
it's not loving like yours.

179

For more than one woman I suffered, I cried.
Oh love how hard you are!
My heart didn't know
taste the value of a female
and flew from flower to flower
looking to find like a hummingbird,
the best of pistils.

180

Twelve years were landless roots,
skin stuck to the bones,

political imprisonment,
torture, bravery,
planned injustice and something else
than the dying homeland.

181

Children are good,
bad are the ones who make them
randomly, without the glory of love.

182

They didn't throw dirt on their corpse,
they set him on fire
and he kept the ashes
of his son in the bleak silence of the injustice.

183

Soon I won't wear my sandals,
the trails won't be the same
with their stones, with the trees,
with the sky and the birds,
with the fragrance of the grass
and nothing and no one will care
destruction of the planet.

184

You settle into my being
and diluted the riddle of feeling
to express that you're real
in the darkness that surrounds us

naked and fearless.

185

The gringo one day had a country
on a distant continent
that it was not called America.

186

Tomorrow I will not justify
the same today:
no ears and no eyes
because on the other side,
I will not fear anymore
god or the devil.

187

Melancholia,
she is a woman in the metaphor,
intimacy of the suicide,
the poison that opens the doors
of a surreal paradise.

189

Marry me I'll teach you
my other half;
you will know that I have
empty pockets and the size
of my heart is heavier
than all the gold of the world.

190

*I was born and nobody lent me
his soul on the tightrope
on the precipice of life.*

191

*The fishes are dead
and the sea is a sewer
where the greed of the nations
developed and powerful
they vomit the poison they have
in its bowels.*

192

*I see in your face, what you will be one day
before being dust: an indifferent
that with ignorance and lies
you made them believe in the myth
of the resurrection.*

193

*I drew love
on the canvas of naivety,
not knowing that it would be
a masterpiece.*

194

*Who will put bells on it
to death when it comes for you,*

so you can breathe another day
on the carousel of life?

195

She expects you to accommodate
the feeling in the spring
of her body where no one ever
dwelt in the paradise of her life.

196

Lie to me if you love me,
don't lie to me if you hate me
because love forgives
and hatred destroys everything.

197

Lean into the lintel of my heart,
I will see your porcelain beauty
slowly seeping into my eyes
where my desire for you capsizes.

198

The poor boy cries
because he has no food
and he doesn't know a Santa Claus
give him toys and treats
in his short and miserable life
and the tears that flow
of the tender eyes of that poor child,
are tears of salt like tears

of a rich boy who sometimes
moans with joy
in a distant country.

199

If someone loved you
how I loved you, I doubt it,
though caresses are plagiarized
and the kisses are repeated
with a man feeling the curves of a woman.

200

How often
we will reproduce the same,
playing love and trying to be free,
doomed to disappear
and never come back.

201

I wish my head would turn
how the world turns,
that my heart did not beat
silent or noisy
like the harmony of eternity.

202

It hurts to forget you,
not remember those things
that did not crash in time

and what did we do looking inside
to the moon hanging out there.

203

Who will read my verses
in this century of mediocrity,
of so many doses of technology
overwhelming and manipulating
to an army of ignorant.

204

I don't know why we call
to our world, Earth,
when we should call it,
the planet of Death.

205

How many bards will I praise
after you and me,
anonymous like pain,
like melancholy
and misunderstanding
of the feeling?

206

A bird in a cage
it's a dead bird:
is like a man
without feet and hands
in a prison.

207

I love your guava essence,
your strawberry lips,
your vanilla beauty
and your coffee soul.

208

Like the wind
my verses slip away
and penetrate deep
and caress when you read them
with the clear waters
of the imagination of your eyes.

209

I love you as you are not:
green on the outside
and blue on the inside,
silver moon, finger ring
of the universe.

210

The birds migrate
they fly like projectiles
piercing the distance
who do not fear and love
because they are freer
that you and me ...

211

You are whirlpool,
creeper, mandrake,
tide, attracting magnet
the positive looking
my negativity.

You are whirlpool,
creeper, mandrake,
tide, attracting magnet
the positive of me,
looking my negativity.

212

Your eyes are fireflies
looking in the dark
the erratic feeling
of those who love each other.

213

A little house
in the sand of a beach,
with its windows and doors open
wants to be a seagull courting the waves
and it is a lover of saltpeter, clouds, space
and it does not moan because it is happy
even if it dies before turning to rubble
from loneliness and try to fly
without having wings…

214

If you get old I will love you:
youth is a fashion outfit
and beauty lays down her trousseau
when the years rape her.

215

I did not choose the office of the bard,
drawing my bow
to shoot an arrow
and not hurt the wind.

216

If I sing it's for you, my muse knows it
because hate did not belong to me,
but if the love, before and after leaving.

217

The bread that serves as a table
and the wine that falls like poison
in the memories to remember
your name, woman.

218

An insect has died
because of indifference
in the streets of loneliness,
and that insect is you.

219

*California has something
that his people do not understand:
its imposing desert, its dirty seas,
its inhospitable nature:
vertebra of the sequoias.*

220

*Covid-19:
State terrorism,
nature attack
against humanity?*

221

*Without you, the possibility is broken
and the impossible is welded
only with the steel of love.*

222

*Love yourself like Dali
loved his donkey with worms, surreal,
 in the gloomy fright of death.*

223

*I see corrupt politicians
that are demagogues, parasites,
inept, thirsty for power,
willing to put down roots
like weeds in Latin American countries.*

224

*Pines grow
like arrows pointing to the sky
with mysticism of the poet's chimeras.*

225

*Morning braids dreams
and the early morning like a virgin
of drooping eyelids,
I make love to her in my nightmares.*

226

*The skein of your arms
catches me,
your feminine countenance,
your breasts, your thighs,
your hips, your buttocks
shaped to perfection of desire,
your sex, -madreselvas-
and I savor your fluids
that circulate like rivers,
like lava from a volcano
coming out of your being.*

227

*The half past 4 lesbian
dresses as a female
and she's looking for a man
to crucify her
as a woman doesn't.*

228

When you miss me
I will not be a nail
in the middle of my finger,
I won't taste you like eggplant
and I'll grow like lichen
in the shadows
of your absence.

229

They invented the axe,
the bow, the arrow, the catapults,
then they created the planes,
tanks, bombs, missiles,
the Coronavirus
in this war of all, of no one.

230

I'll stop lying if I love you.
And I'll be less of a man
when you're not mine.

231

The rivulet has a smile
and own voice, rhyme, and sing
and is slowly dying
on the earth,
when it stretches
getting lost in the distance.

232

I'm not the shoe soles anymore,
weigh the paths of ostracism,
how love and hatred weigh.

233

I ran out of ropes,
without intonating the truth
because I ran out of echoes,
of the rhetoric of insomnia,
listening to the shit that reproduces
communist dictators,
Democratic demagogues in the US
and the corrupt socialists in Latin America.

234

Love Hurts,
unites, disintegrates,
it is yeast, gall, honey,
pain, pleasure,
and a brittle bridge.

235

The sensuality slides
on the cliff of meat
where every part of humanity
go down and up,
shrink and lengthen
In the hell of desire.

236

I say goodbye to my enemies
of my first love
of infertility that defines men.

237

I love you California, -a part of you-
where your streams, your tributaries,
rivers, lakes, mountains and hills,
with their curtains of greenery
invite me to dream,
to get away from everyday life.

238

She is not a poem,
she is less than a kiss
on the precipice of dawn
when we make love.

239

Keep my hands
so you can fly
with the imagination
and the deception of the poet.

240

I'm terrified of the dawn
with its explosion of nuances
challenging my eyes.

241

Stay with the dead man I am,
I won't nail hate
at the carnivals of happiness.

242

With the debt of your love
and the interests of your kisses,
you turned me into an owl
and I stay up late in the endless nudity
of your being.

243

The day walks in the bars
from the prison of this world
counting the time of the living
and the eternity of the dead.

244

The drums of the river
sing the notes of spring
and the breeze in your mouth is a waterfall,
a dancer who tramples the heart.

245

My pug is waiting for me in my absence of slave
and with the smile of his tail
and the flat face of him,
he softens the best of me when I comes home.

246

Don't go mother,
don't leave me,
that your belly sings
the love we all need.

247

Step like a zero
when you're with me
and you subtract yourself as the best number
in the neurons of memories.

248

If I'm well hurt,
If I tell the truth I'm another anti-Christ,
if I give up how little I have
they watch me as the wretched ones who are...

249

Let the pines sing my land,
they sing with their high notes
in the summer and fall
of your heart and mine.

250

Woman lend me what I want:
the drums of your buttocks,
your guitar hips
to become the music

that I have inside and in the rhythm
that this man wears on the outside.

251

Our hands are butterflies
in the spring garden
of our naked bodies, off and on
at night and at every dawn.

252

I raised the anchor and set sail
to never come back
to the port where one day
your lips kissed me
promising me the mainland
and not the sea that melts
with the sky, there, there, in the distance.

253

Again the dust of oblivion
falls silently on the table,
while like the last fruit
of the sin that brought us back to life.

254

You're more meek
that a lamb's neck
handing himself
over to the edge of the knife,
more docile than rain

rushing over the rocks
that soften your love and mine.

255

Palms try to kiss the sky
and they just caress the wind
that make them feel
leaner, more beautiful. and greener.

256

They don't know that hunger,
corruption, wars and conflicts
murder hundreds and thousands of children,
with your complicity and mine,
with the mutism of indifference
that discreetly aborts humanity.

257

Prisons should not exist,
nor should governments,
nor borders, nor armies,
nor police, nor so many laws,
nor so many judges,
if we were better,
without dividing everything in the name
of love and hate,
of God and the Devil.

258

Light me up with your eyes
the passageways of love,

who are long and intricate
and let me fly with your hands
when you caress me
in our universe of the two.

259

Anything that happens
in the winter or summer,
not in the fictional part of autumn
nor in the spring loop.

260

I love the thorns of flowers,
not its fragile and perishable petals.

261

The birds won't come back, I know that.
I'll miss their the gorges
in twilight and at dawn;
their peaks piercing the distance
with the flapping of your flights and I will condemn
to those guilty of our misfortune
by the last endangered species.

262

Nobody's going to tell me I lost you
for not having more time
to assemble the pieces of my body
I left on the paths of the years.

263

I don't deny that I jumped more than once
of the suicide trampoline.

264

Who will take care of you
when you are abandoned
the ones you thought loved you
more than I did?

265

I renounce the treacherous anchor,
to the terrorist hook
and not to the bait of your love
fishing my manhood
by the desire of a woman.

266

The lichens withered
when they stole the shadows
in the desert of melancholy.

267

The bells fell silent,
cut their tongues of clappers
died with the centuries
and few remember
that they existed
when we were more beasts and less human.

268

Mine is worth it,
without legs or head, hovering
where tragic loves hide.

269

The feeling of incapacity
settles in the caverns of exhaustion
and flees from the pits of fear
to discover that the life is a scaffold
in the enormous prison of this planet.

270

The giraffe of my dreams
killed the last hunter
-animal killer-
and hung him
with his rifle in a tree
in faraway Africa.

271

I am still crying for the death of my mother.
And others who still have her alive
do not weep for her and make her suffer.

272

The early flowers
give themselves to the sun
they commit suicide with the wind

for letting you love
as I love you.

273

Icy wind,
burning breeze:
Why do you go away
and why do you come back
in the cold winter
and in the monotonous summer
like a wanderer
wandering
in the roundness of the earth?

274

Eyelids swollen
like the candles of the moon
and your tongue captive
and wet in your mouth
speaks truths
and exclaims lies.

275

I fell in love
with delicacy and beauty
of your petals
and you stuck
your thorns in me
not in the heart,
but in the soul.

276

*I will come looking for you to be mine
and I will kidnap the desire that imposes
to the mortals all that fits
in the universe of your body, woman.*

277

*I am afraid to live and not to die
because before being born I was already dead.*

278

*Always the same
in the history of Latin America:
corrupt governments,
socialist dictatorships,
poverty clogging the asses
with the cobwebs of hunger.*

279

*Light I see you
in the brevity of existence,
darkness that I feel
in the infinity of the universe.*

280

*Spring feels cold
burying the autumn
like the corpses
after being cremated.*

281

*Wake me up with the butterflies
of your lips fluttering
over my desire ignited with your love.*

282

*Don't go away so early
if you go don't leave me at dawn
I'm about to detonate
without your love.*

283

*Widen your heart
enter "rumbeando"
through the doors of the soul
and dance showing
the best of you.*

284

*If I lack water
let me have more light
and if everything is darkened
I will live in freedom.*

285

*My tongue abhors
the cell of my mouth
the bars of my teeth.*

286

If I were to sing to you
it would be for the tenderness
that your essence has in abundance
and for the subtlety of your being.

287

Come, let the stones
speak to us with their silence
as love does.

288

They went away defeated by the time
betrayed by existence,
as you and I will leave someday.

289

The children frolic
they grow and soar
like trees
fragile and robust
in the jungle of life.

290

The garden is awake
sunflowers kiss the sun
and the flowers know
how to caress the wind.

291

Today I write in the morning
my best verses
imitating the dew, the grass
unloading the colors
of this dawn
while your absence
soaks the pain I feel
for having lost you forever.

292

Let's play at being children
and not to be men
because there is nothing
better and more beautiful
than innocence
and daydreaming.

293

Your truth and mine
what are they good for:
To build walls,
to open trenches,
to invent frontiers
and divide mankind?

294

My foam, the foam of the seas
my water, that of the rivers,
my freedom: my verse,

*his lips, my wine
a piece of bread on the table
and breathe without fear.*

295

*Yesterday he was shot
the soldiers of the dictatorship.
His crime was to think differently
and to fall in love with the freedom
that tyrants hate.*

296

*When a starving child dies
in misery, in poverty:
Whom do we blame afterward?
Whom do we condemn?
You, me, everyone?*

297

*With the lights of hatred
wars are made
conflicts are manufactured
mutilating one more piece
of what we still have left
of peace and love.*

298

*I remember you as a shell
with the taste of egg and lemon
on the palate of innocence.*

299

Before murdering them
humiliate and torture them,
in what a way!
And all for the cruelty of bullfighting.

300
In the brief space of two
galaxies of hearts fit,
firmaments of caresses
and the freedom to believe in the art of love.

301

Love is more powerful than hate,
because love is the art of peace
and hate the mediocrity
of those who do not give love
and who pretend to love.

302

With suffering and pain
I will make my banners
and with joy and love
the boundaries that do not divide
countries and peoples.

303

By the clear edges of the moon
walk your eyes and mine

*in love with things
that do not fit in the feeling.*

304

*What could I give you
that would be worth more than your life
than the erratic verse of the poet
stumbling through the streets
of love and hate?*

305

*Turning I found you and you were so wide
that your love overflowed the pitchers of my soul.*

306

*I place the pieces of your body
in the puzzle of passion
and I put you together where love
is not alms, forgiveness, nor sin.*

307

*If you came back, I would lull you to sleep
with the sheets of the night
and with my skin, I would make you
the best wedding dress.*

308

*Your eyes are, what are your eyes?
Two moons or suns in your face?*

309

To stay because if we go away again
if they take away our life,
if they take away everything...

310

I promise you that I will love you
with a plus and a minus
exceeding and emptying myself
by loving us so much.

311

The rocks speak to me
because of how dead they are
they speak to me that they were alive
once in the destructive
landscape of this world.

312

They are drops of water
that descend
from the vessels of the sky,
melodic rain
of all times.

313

They are lips that burn,
that hurt like ice,
kisses of paper and spines,

wet and dry kisses
that promise so much and nothing,
that close the eyes
and open the gates of the heart
with the inexplicable stampede of love.

314

The bar and your woman's smile,
my masculinity printing notes,
the sound of tongues
trapped in the bars of teeth,
weaving fantasies
between alcohol and drugs
and everyone seems to know each other
pretending to be friends,
believing in the altars
of fictitious happiness
and not in latent hatred.

315

He died young and nobody killed him
from the front or from behind with a stab;
he was eaten from within in silence and slowly
what they call cancer.

316

Where will I find so much to love you
after having given you everything
and you have given me more
than what is not enough for you?

317

Those who return and leave
fear to die like plants
on the edges of the road.

318

We pass like the seconds,
increasing the interests to live,
preparing in our noses
the coffins of death.

319
You sleep and you go
I don't know where
and I would like to look for you
even if I get lost in the labyrinth
of your dreams.

320

Not a word less
not a word too much:
you have said it all
with your verses, poetry.

321

With what eyes will you look at me
when I stumble and fall
into the abyss of death?

322

Your salty tears
are tears of sorrow, of joy and fear,
and they renounce what we feel inside and out.

323

That child closed his eyelids,
he wanted to sleep forever
tired of living alienated
in his surrealistic country
with so much poverty and misery.

324

Anchor, don't throw yourself into the water
that the sailboat tries to hoist the sails
and fly over the waves like a seagull
on the immense sea.

325

They flee their countries
because of injustice,
because of corrupt governments,
because of socialist dictatorships
and like anonymous shadows
they seek the American dream.

326

Without so much, I give my best
my steps know it

and the dust of the roads
that my bones implore.

327

If you mock me
it is because your eyes
do not hide your tongue
in the dungeon of your mouth.

328

If we are blamed for everything,
we will survive
among the gleanings,
hidden in the petals of the flowers
in the garden of injustice.

329

Mother I miss you so much
that in the altarpiece of memories
grow the roses that I sowed for you.

330

The pieces of the chessboard
the music of victory and defeat
between two players who begin
to hate each other without being enemies.

331

They are all born,

they grow, they multiply,
they cry, laugh and die
in the loop of life, all, all...

332

You undress me with your smile
you undress me with your eyes
and after meeting you in intimacy
I live without clothes and thanks to you.

333

She lacked nothing
nothing to her beauty
and she died of love
because nobody loved her.

334

She was born prematurely
she grew prematurely
and died prematurely
without understanding the reasons
of love and hate.

335

Waves don't go away,
come back that I love you
and it hurts me to see you
commit suicide
on the reefs, on the cliffs

and in the sands of the beach.

336

Who are we
if we annihilate the animals
if we destroy the forests
the atmosphere, the seas, the rivers
rivers and natural resources?

337

Turn off the lights
that clashes
with clarity
and collide with me
in the darkness
with the sensual edges
of your body, girl.

338

My other half
knows more about you
than my other half
more human.

339

I will leave the invisible art
of poetry and I will begin
to sculpt your beauty
where love belongs.

340

*Pumpkins are made with eyes,
noses and mouths on Halloween
and the gringos don't know
that millions of pumpkins
with no eyes, no noses and no mouths
could save millions of children
who are dying of starvation.*

341

*The prison devours men,
it is not a just punishment
for the innocent,
nor is it a good prison
for animals.*

342

*The palms kiss the heaven,
in love with the breeze
they stretch and dance
on the catwalk of the space.*

343

*I fear the dead more
than the living that I am
when I still think and I am asleep.*

344

Remember not the branches, the sturdy trees,

remember the dust and also the earth
and what they are made of.

345

I am alone, we are alone
and we know that at the end of life death
will devour us with macabre style.

346

Seek the creator of injustice,
of manipulation and chaos,
many will not be afraid
and will say that he is God.

347

The ant fell asleep
therefore work, received no salary
and lost everything away from the anthill.

348

The woman I love
has not yet been born
because she is still dead
like the corpse
that oblivion has not aborted

349

I need, what do I need?
To love like a few

and to hate like the others?

350

Our cruelty
is not a meek cruelty
it is the worst cruelty of all beasts.

351

They manipulate us and divide
among themselves the riches.
And they make us poorer in order to divide us
as peoples without identity.

352

I will know how to lose and not win
to live in peace and not in war
and poetry will be the pin
that sticks in the flesh
of those who hate and destroy.

353

The beggars multiply
they do not cry for you nor for me
they settle in the streets
where they fear to sleep the slaves
of the governments.

354

To be free is to have identity

is not to believe, is to know how to doubt
to think, to love and not to hate.

355

God and the Devil do not hide
from humanity the truth of everything
because they have never existed.

356

We are condemned to die
and although I do not understand why
I would like to elucidate that our world
is a machinery that destroys everything.

357

I gave you my white roses out of time
and you gave me the red petals of the heart.

358

I can lose my teeth
my eyes, the worst or the best of me
but I will remain without imitating
the fashion of men.

359

In the end, there will be no sea
rivers, lakes, forests
beasts, nor atmosphere
and we will be the last endangered species.

360

*In chaos we are born
and we will continue to die
because we are primitive creatures.*

361

*The grass is so green
that it allows itself to be eaten
like the men who eat
all the animals.*

362

*Your calamity is not mine
nor your piercing pain
the misfortune of the people.*

363

*Stay with me tonight
no one will know
how we will turn off the light
and take off our clothes
with the hands of the soul.*

364

*A free bird pecks at my ear
and every day
I detest more and more
the songs of the humanity.*

365

In the forge of hatred
of selfishness, of hypocrisy
of injustice, of power
and demagogy, politicians grow up
deceiving many, but not all.

366

Make me grow from within
with deep roots
that touch your heart
so that love may sprout
in the space occupied by hate.

367

I would like to give you my poetry
what you do not have,
what they have taken from you
to reduce your poverty,
to cut in pieces the injustice
and to distribute it
among those who prolong
for centuries the misfortune
of the peoples.

368

At what hour will you come
to give me what I need
and grow after loving you?

369

Come on, muses!
I love you in my delirium
of poet with sea and without land.

370

You weep for him and the fashion of your mourning
settles in your beauty
and you do not know that the man
that I am would like to take his place.

371

My cat Resfalgio
played with the ball of the moon
and ate the stars
thinking they were fish
in the ocean of darkness.

372

Tomorrow I will become
dust and the best of me
will fly in the pages
of a book where my verses
will eternalize what I was
and what I will be forever.

373

Why do you put price your body

and you sell yourself
where the predators of desire
will undermine your flesh
and what is left of you?

374

Where the dirty waters
and the clean waters will go
like the dead and the living when they mix?

375

It's all a continuity
in the carousel of nature,
programming what moves and exists
in the cage of this planet.

376

Out of you, I'm not the same, Mother,
because you didn't teach me
to love or hate in the paradise of your womb.

377

In the burrow of your eyes
love doesn't need roots, earth and fertilizer.

378

The man that I am
has not ceased to be a child
when he loves you

running naked through the streets
and the avenues of your body

379

They no longer throw dirt on the dead
they cremate him, their ashes flying around
like cursed crows
or they rest bottled up in any place
condemned not to be free.

380

Woman, the insect that I am
does not sleep early
in the jungle of your body.

381

With perfection the roses grow,
and with love, everything germinates

382

The corpse that is not a mummy
has much space in its narrow coffin
and waits to look at us with empty eyes
pronouncing today's death.

383

There are mountains of sand
that did not want to be mounds
of stones or rocks and defy gravity

mocking the nature of the living.

384

*We have changed
as the teeth change
the hands, the hairs
and the symphony of the skin
with its wrinkled notes.*

385

*No one will bring you back:
Neither justice nor love,
nor innocence, nor goodness,
nor gods, nor demons
because death condemns,
as ignorance condemns
to primitive creatures.*

386

*Seek the drug,
inject it, smoke it, or swallow it,
try to avoid reality,
to escape from the dungeon of your body
and from the huge cell of this world.*

387

*No one will denounce the silence
nor the cry of injustice,*

nor those who come,
nor those who will go after…

388

It was, what was it?
The shadow on the broken shoes,
the hunger under the ribs,
the poor child, as poor
are the peoples: the broken and weary plow
of the earth's sharp teeth?

389

In love with the sun and the sky
I raised kites in La Havana,
and believed he was free without being so,
a bird in a revolutionary cage,
fantasies that capsized in my innocence.

390

My dreams were not bigger than yours,
but my nightmares were:
at the age of 17, I was condemned for loving freedom
that I didn't have and that was stolen from my people
in the name of socialism and a fictitious revolution.

391

What are we
when we are asleep,
filled inside, empty on the outside?
What are we in the daytime when we're awake

*and we forget to dream
without caring about anything?*

392

*There's a belly out there.
pregnant with pollen,
it's spring who starts to give birth
their best children.*

394

*I wanted his face, not mine,
her beauty hanging on my eyelids
and I fell short of love
that she gave away.*

395

*There is a swarm of bees
in the apiary of desire
that sweeten life
even if men castrate
the honey of love.*

396

*From sadness, joy is born,
out of broken illusions, hope,
and from the poverty and injustice
of peoples, love arises.*

397

I see you passing by so pretty
and stretched out,
dancing in time,
with your forms and emotions
that makes me think that the sublime
is fragile petal, limpid water,
brittle space in a picture hanging on the wall.

398

I starch you with the semen
of my pauper testicles,
painting the walls of your body
and you ask me for more by climbing
on the mast of my virility
to sail where nothing is forbidden.

399

She is a work of art,
she gives herself for the love
of the dew wetting the grass,
like the waterfall defying
gravity in its fall,
like summer and winter
that never coincide.

400

How many women have arrived
and have already left?
And how many have I lowered the stars

when it was day or night
improvising my love poems?

401

Tonight you will be mine
no matter what it takes
to poison the feeling
to do such things,
that a man does to a woman.

402

You were all mine
and I without being yours
I refused to put
the noose around my neck.

403

The north wind
sleeps out there
and I specter in the daybreak
I make love to my pillow,
while the pen bleeds
my verses for you...

404

What you give me
does not fit in my heart,
I place it in my neurons
so as never to forget you.

405

She has what I want,
without secrets, without pomp
no fuss, no colorfulness,
light and deep,
like her kisses:
root of tenderness.

406

With the years everything passes,
no one remains as a seed;
without realizing
that death hides under the nails.

407

I see you changed, with the same eyes
that yesterday looked at your porcelain face
today turned into a cracked canvas.

408

They will tell me that you are not there,
that you ran away
because of love and not hate.

409

The lies that are born
inside are sown
in the orchards of wickedness.

410

*I tried to leave her
as you stop dreaming,
to be joyful and to love
in the world of monotony.*

411

*I'll stay like a burnt-out light bulb
waiting for you to light with your fingers
the fire of my heart.*

412

*Palms cry
when the fingers of the storm
caress their slender necks
and they seem like they will break
tired of so many caresses.*

413

*Rain. The wet earth
smells of life, death
and the sharp and dangerous winter
stabs us in the back.*

414

*The crystalline waters
and the dirty waters
mingle as men
mix the feeling.*

415

*In blue and white
you dress and you also undress:
in blue and white...*

416

*Living without fear
of the creation of the Covid-19,
of an autumn turned into summer,
of a corrupt democracy,
of a socialist dictatorship,
of a god and so many demons,
of love and hate...*

417

*I arrived like my parents, brothers and sisters,
as my ancestors were born
and I will die as the children of mankind:
exterminated century after century
in the game of life and death
and ironically many still believe
in the myths of gods, demons
and in so many tyrannical and manipulative prophets.*

418

*No one will wait for you,
neither those who loved you,
nor those who hated you afterward,
digging tombs in the hills
of peace and war.*

419

I do not rhyme my verse because it lacks
what is absent in the poetry of some bards
who read their poems in the deaf ears of the peoples.

420

On the ruins of the past
the bare feet of the child I was
run through the squares and avenues
of my third world country.

421

I cry over the tombstone of indifference
and my tears bounce
on the foundations of pain
for having lost her forever.

422

My adolescence was murdered
as they assassinated Miguel Hernandez,
Juan Clemente Zenea and Lorca,
the henchmen of a tyranny,
but they let me live for fear
of becoming the youngest martyr
of the political prison.

423

Those who stayed put down roots,
multiplied like weeds.

424

Today I breathe, work and walk.
I give love as they give hate
and in the streets of perdition
I am anything, but what you are.

425

Your eyes and mine
roll in the night
and jump for joy
at every morning.

426

What are you life?
What are you death?
Creation of a tyrannical god
or the brutal manifestation of nature?

427

Small is my heart,
my hands and what I offer with love
does not charge with the interests of hatred
because the essence of my verses
fits in the subject of the lovers.

428

The sad child was born
as the children are born:
he was born naked.

429

I could dream
with my eyes open
and without being
a slave to my dreams
I stayed up all night
looking for you, poetry.

430

Yesterday the melancholy was different:
drizzle, dew, snow, waterfall,
waves, tide, current, what do I know?

431

The campaigns fell silent,
their tongues of clappers
melted with the time to hate
thanks to the justice of men.

432

To be dead is to return to the beyond,
not to return here, to break the anchor:
a shot in eternity.

433

We walk in the curvature of the world,
without caring to see
the abyss that exists
so close to you and me.

434

What do we have inside, mother?
An insatiable beast,
a sleeping monster, an alien
thirsty for love, for hate,
of everything that exists
on this planet to satisfy
our survival instinct?

435

That comet passed over our heads,
mysticism in the unfathomable abyss
of the universe
to remind us that to live trapped
in the sphere of our world,
is synonymous with death.

436

I will run out of dreams,
the routine of loving, the daily longing,
the anxiety of existing, of feeling the steps
on the dust of the roads
and don't say that I was a coward.

437

Spins, everything spins
in the darkness of the eternal night
and it is the fantasy of the light
an opener that penetrates the eyes.

438

I would like to sing to you with my voice
and not with the silence of my verses,
I would like to give you love without my arms,
to caress you without my fingers,
but I don't understand those things
that above the skin and the heart,
crash, succumb and are shipwrecked...

439

Spain, beautiful land,
your musical geography
is a deep song,
disgrace of the murdered poet
and of the bard in exile.

440

I eat the flesh of a murdered animal
because everybody does it to subsist
without caring to be more beasts
than all the beasts.

441

What did my father teach me?
To hate, to love, to forgive,
to not be afraid, to live,
to be more of a man, more of a womanizer,
to share a piece of bread,
not to steal, to doubt and not to believe?

442

It rains. That scent of wet earth,
of naked grass, of drowned petals,
the trees without umbrellas,
the breeze shattering windows,
the shady ferns,
to ripe fruits afraid detach from the branches,
to the roofs of the houses and to the ground
intoning those melodies
in this February downpour,
they make me vibrate with infinite nostalgia
in the exile consecrated to melancholy.

443

You won't come back, I know it...!
Although I kept all
what tears love apart
when light of baggage
I left breaking
the best of you and me.

444

With the sweat of the brow
 the bread arrives to the hands of the worker
and with cowardice they dress themselves,
those who neither bleed nor sweat.

445

I wanted to be young when I got tired
of counting the steps of the years.

446

I learned to live and discovered
tears without cheeks, cheeks without tears
falling in deserted corners.

447

The sound of the prison bars
is the melody that a prisoner
will never forget.

448

Now I think of death more than yesterday.
Could it be because I don't believe,
because I stopped hating
and I opened the closet where we hide
the secrets that condemned us one day?

449

Poor us all.
Ephemeris, carnivals,
an old year, a new year,
abortions, births,
the improvisation of something,
mediocrity turned into art.

450

Noontime asked me
where was the last tooth
that killed my worst cavities.

451

I see what I shouldn't have looked at.
Hungry children, children without clothes,
children dressed in the skin of innocence;
children who die as children,
children who will remain
killed in countries where corruption
and injustice go hand in hand.

452

Do not expect to read my poetry easily
because my verses are bullets,
burning arrows
and poisoned darts
for the enemy who
to his brother and mother
did not stretch out his hand
to say: "I love you!

453

Who will put his heart
in the tray of desire
and with his eyes will he not look
and with his ears will he not hear
to lust, to wickedness,
to his fathers and brothers
for love embraces all things?

454

I do not believe in you because to live is to die

and to suffer, while we breathe
with the miserable quota of existing
in the enormous prison that is the Earth.

455

Give me neither love nor hate,
I don't need it.
Give me the humanity
that people lack.

456

I pretend to remember you
as you were when time
did not crash on your face.

457

The deceased of today
is the same dead of yesterday,
he is not changed by fashion,
by science, by technology,
neither by the governments.

458

Of love poems
and verses without soul
born what you feel
if you cry, if you laugh, if you sing,
with or without the identity
that they steal from us to turn us
into obedient slaves.

126

459

The birds flee,
they migrate, they soak the space,
and me, I neither migrate nor fly,
because I have roots
that bind me to the earth,
as the sea binds the sailor.

460

The years accumulate
charging us the interest
of death because we are
and we will be debtors for living,
for loving, hating and thinking.

461

I have not loved so much because of fear,
I was not free because I was a coward,
because I followed the rhythm of the peoples
along the paths of silence
and indifference.

462

My beaches with their clear waters
with their fine sand and blue sky,
are there, in my memories,
in the tropic of the Caribbean
of my happy and languid island,
where exile did not dare
to close the curtains of memories.

463

Why lie
if the truth is deep and rests
as nothing and nobody does?

464

The widow dresses in mourning
and now she is more beautiful
by inside than outside.

465

My brother went away
without saying goodbye.
I was convinced that in the tedium
of the sunsets
wrote his best verses.

466

I keep the thorns
of fish and roses,
because simulated love
hurts more than all the thorns.

467

Chanting I go in silence
and imitating my footsteps
through the paths of life
where men are lost.

468

Listen to the waves
when they crash
against the rocks,
hear the sound of the wind
improvising on the branches
of the trees those notes
unforgettable and divine,
perceives the rain
when it splashes on the floors:
Have you ever heard
more sublime melodies
and perfect ones that make you dream
awake and asleep?

469

Foul autumn you dress yourself in gold
with the pain of the leaves
when they wither and jump
from the trees with the complicity
of the breeze.

470

We all hope in the row of time
what we have to do of the wretched
of existence.

471

We eat cows, pigs,
birds, fish, dogs, cats,

seafood, insects, -what do I know?-
Yes, we devoured everything
that exists in the habitat of our world!
And what are we, humanity?
Parasites, viruses, bacteria…
Are we worse than the beasts?

472

What a calamity of the present
when the years go by
and accumulate weighing us down,
without caring about the past and the future
of what we have lived,
stabbing us in the front or in the back
with the dagger of time.

473

I will remember you
as one does not forget
the first love,
the wound that does not heal the feeling.

474

History repeats itself:
abortions of dictatorships,
bloody revolutions,
the scam of socialism,
corrupt governments,
ferocious capitalism
and democracy turned
into an organized mafia.

475

Open love,
Let me in
through your windows,
not through your doors,
I'm the thief of desire.

476

What is difficult about you
is narrowed in the wide,
it's hard to bring it afloat
in the ocean
of incomprehension.

477

They divide us, manipulate
and subjugate us
ever since the peoples
have contracted nuptials
with humanity.

478

Your best parts
serve as spare parts
to my manhood.

479

I tried to sleep early,
to get up after sunrise

and addicted to sleep,
my verses with you or without you,
banish me from your dreams.

480

Let us blame god and the devil
for our eternal misfortune
and for the first time, we will be free
and not slaves to the fear
caused by manipulation and ignorance.

481

I will buy poverty from the rich
and at least I will think
that it will no longer subsist
in the atrocious reality of our world.

482

That woman fills me inside,
she emptied me on the outside
and her love still hurts me.

483

Twists and turns that carry us
and move us to where in the infinite?

484

My house, cradle of my body
protects me from the cold, from the heat,

from the night and the day,
and I neither sing to it
nor worship it in my verses.

485

There is always my faithful friend,
my dog, with his smile on his tail,
barking at the birds,
jumping over the sun and the moon,
waiting for a caress
and a bone made with love.

486

The seagulls,
masters of the sky,
as free as their light wings,
they love the sea, as I love you.

487

That lantern in the darkness
with its dim light opening
the space of the night
in the street of loneliness,
witnessed my first kiss
on the lips of love.

488

Something of me
fertilizes your body,
water your beauty,

cultivates in your breast
the fruits of the dawn.

489

I would not like to write you
an ode to your being, my beloved,
nor a hymn to happiness
that sublimates you better,
because nothing and no one
compensates your infinite love.

490

Memorize how you feel
when it eats you inside
the famine, the misery, the poverty,
living in a country
where you should never have been born.

491

Tell me a story
that begins with death
and not with the fable of existence.

492

The cat has diamond eyes
and they shine in the darkness
like two pearls that stalk
death.

493

No one will tell me
what I have to do
if I love less, if I hate more.

494

Our poems
will be worthless,
when everything passes away
as fashion passes,
technology,
war and peace.

495

I ruin what I touch,
I compose in the air
and I build with my hands
and not with the heart.

496

So much to say for what
if what hurts the least
will not make you cry,
if with love and hate
the temples of faith are built.

497

This man that I am,
ceased to be a child,

he became an old man
and in laughing skeleton.

498

Inevitable is not to die,
it is not to be eternal,
it is to leave the prison of this world
and of the body that traps us,
that sentences us.

499

I am your victim
when you undress me
and I pretend to love you
as you love me.

500

Your works like the leftovers
that the poor eat
to fill their empty stomachs,
are works that will be admired
by your flatterers
and your army of hypocrites.

There is a train...

There is a freight train
that is the train of death for many
and the train of dreams for others.
A train that crosses the distance,
rolling on its rails, hundreds of miles.
They call it The Beast;
it is a train that outlines fear and insecurity
and passes with the noise of its steel wheels
through every town where history is a sad story
and that train like a wild bull, made of metal,
does not transport pain and misery,
but it does transport the people
who flee their nations because of corrupt governments
of socialist dictatorships,
of fictitious democracy
with its gangs of drug traffickers and organized mafias,
peoples who migrate like anonymous shadows
illegally to the United States
on the train called La Bestia (The Beast),
in search of freedom,
prosperity and justice
they never had in the country they were born.

I don't remember.

I don't remember the last time
I masturbated writing your name
on the walls of the political prison,
memorizing your legs,
your tight thighs,
the nudity of your geography,
your beauty detonating in my senses
on those nights of two,
when your sex like a flower
allowed the mast of my manhood
sail in your essence,
without reaching the port where
love was over,
but where the desire began
of a man for a woman...

Sometimes...

Sometimes
the reminiscence
is a raven that perches
in the grids of the eyes,
while this torrid heat
melts the icebergs that hold me up
on the cliff of fate
and the infant I was,
still seeks the man I am
regardless of the stench
in the dumps of love and hate.

After so much...

141

After so much,
of little, of hanging the spring
without pictures,
of liquefying seasons,
of seeing the leaves languishing
on the lintels of boredom
and the pines mourning
in the harshest winter
with a mystical white
on the hillsides,
on the plains, on the mountains,
no one will change anything,
neither your years nor mine...

Yesterday.

Yesterday the stillness dug tunnels
furrows, graves, holes,
squandering the pain of political imprisonment
in the hell of my island called paradise,
in my country turned into the Gulag of the Americas,
in an enormous "passive" extermination camp,
where they buried and still entomb
the living, who loved the freedom
without remembering the dead of yesterday and today
sentenced with the golden injustice of the proletariat.
the injustice of the proletariat.

And we were many Cubans,
-hundreds, thousands, millions,-
imprisoned for not being afraid,
decades after decades,
-rebels, brothers, friends,
families, patriots, Martians-
for trying to be free,
empty and full as the vases
of courage and truth,
sketching love in pain,
passion in despair.
and a dream of freedom that will not come to an end
in the history of oppressed peoples.

*When love does not nest
it is because it has wings to spare
to fly low, from branch to branch,
and flutter high, from cloud to cloud,
searching in the skin of the breeze
the best kisses.*

*And there where desire and innocence
desire and innocence,
the evening falls in love with the night,
the sea of the sky,
the mountains of space,
the seas of the clouds,
the rivers of the earth
and the creatures of the world
admire the subtle and
subtle and sinister colors of nature
after the day's end.*

With your hands and mine.

With your hands and mine,
what would we not do, love,
what would we not do in the present and not tomorrow!
Rebuild what is destroyed,
repair what is broken
inside the crystals of the soul,
empty the ocean of sadness
so as not to run aground in indifference
and embroider the twilight with kisses
that joins legs with legs,
arms with arms, breasts with breasts,
hair with hair,
eyes with eyes, fluids with fluids,
sex with sex?
And what if everything is transformed
in our absence,
to paint blue and not black,
yellow and not red, our universe
and where the horizon begins and ends,
let no one divide the planet with the frontiers
of hatred, of wars,
of inequalities and injustice
because humanity is more than a country,
more than a continent, more than a people,
than a language, than a religion, than a culture,
than a god, than a demon,
than a fatherland and a flag.

And the years go by
like a tornado,
like rain and a squall
and love matures and rots
with the apathy of growing,
of throwing branches, useless roots,
without understanding that the brevity
of breathing can do more than pride,
than vanity, envy,
than incomprehension,
that everything frivolous and unfathomable
that we sometimes feel,
before and after loving each other.

I describe.

I describe the cadence of the air
in the perplexity of my verses
and with the vigil of my prose
I desire today more than yesterday
your origami kisses
in the intimacy of feeling
what fits in the crossword puzzle of life and death
and though the past is as mortal
as flesh and bones,
it hides in silence
and germinates and sprouts discreetly
what we repeat one day
without fear and with anxiety
until the last century.

I am not a poet.

I am not a poet
nor do I want to be,
he said nostalgically
to indifference
and the scent of January
listening to the music
with its invisible notes,
rhymed the melancholy
in the serene night
and made me believe
in the terrifying sorrow
experienced by bards
when they lose themselves anonymously
in the labyrinths of joy.

Do not bleed...

Do not bleed for his love,
it's not worth it, woman,
it is not worth it because the hearts
of men are hard as stones
and fragile as petals
and they beat without hearing the resonances
that they compose in the chest
and the feeling if it is not a broken wing
perches like a hummingbird,
from rose to rose,
to drink the nectar of desire
and savor it all
with the extension of the passion
that embraces the evening of those who love each other
without asking the morning's permission,
even if they dawn later empty inside
and naked on the outside...

You are so beautiful.

You are so beautiful
that youth tastes
the best of you
and you don't understand it
because you are far
from being dust and not seed.

You are so subtle and serene
that seeing you reminds me that spring
does not end when summer arrives
with its parade of colors,
with its original scent
on the background of the afternoon
because you symbolize the curves
of a Spanish guitar,
dancer in a temple
of bubble and rice,
mimic of the horizon,
eyes of the sun, pale moon
that travels amused
through my being,
like time
that goes through everything.

Your love floats...

Your love floats sensitive
to those who travel
without being tourists or pilgrims
where the distance
in the curvature
of a female's lips
defies space,
imitates the geometry of the world
and disputes the gravity
of the broken feeling,
the penultimate tear
outlining oceans
in the twilight of two.

Outside...

Outside the ground
is dressed as a bride,
the pines sing of the insecurity of the north winds
and your caresses rain down
cushioning the cruelty of winter.

Today what was yesterday is so small
that it does not fit in the memories
and each anniversary is a sentence
that ascends and descends in equilibrium
on the edge of the daggers of the years.

Melancholy close your peak
and let me fly
that this blue and black sky
mourns what it touches in the Nevada desert
where my feet know more of my exile
than of my hands...!

The room.

The room accommodates the insomnia
on the sofa of my soul and my bones,
-clotheslines beneath my dermis, -
support the pentagram of my life.
And this body I possess,
-agglutination of old age,
unfinished youth,-
is a mast without a sail that extends
in the topography of my corpse
searching in the oceans of darkness,
the contours of courage and not of fear.

At this moment I would not like to write
of love or hate,
I would like to innovate verses without souls,
without the approval of my muse
so as not to feel the malice growing
in the garbage dumps of the peoples
and to see with only one eye the abyss
of my universe that would serve me
to feel the eternity of death
and at least I would believe in something different.

Awake. The same thing again:
the amalgam of peoples,
the repetition of the everyday
wars, conflicts, less love and more hate, borders
barbed wire fences, walls, firing squads, prisons,
the gallows of inequalities,
socialist dictatorships, artificial democracies,
mafias turned into governments
and the greed of mankind with its pockets torn open:
toothless women prostituted politicians,
judges without dignity,
unsatisfied virgins, buffoons who are magistrates,
manipulated drug addicts, lawyers of evil,
pedophile presidents, genocidal diplomats,
masks, religion, fashion, rich and poor,
corruption and injustice, while someone
who dreams differently, far away,
is a sad, barefooted, and naked child
who does not grow by day or night
and wears the innocence, -flesh of injustice-
dying in third worlds
for nobody's fault, for everybody's fault...

Without being an ostrich...

Without being an ostrich I sink my head
halfway down my neck
in the mud of indifference.

I would try to escape from the flesh
and I would not want to become dust,
into ashes, into dung,
into the recyclable matter;
to get out of the cage of my bones,
to escape from the prison of this planet,
-machinery that destroys everything-,
but I feel the same as you do,
but I feel the same as you,
without believing, without stealing identity,
not clinging to the earth,
to the fruit, to the seed,
to the money, to the gold,
to the subtle shine of the diamond
and forgetting in the sunrise
I dissipate in the twilight
that exists neither before nor after
of being born and dying.

I fear...

I fear to think and I am not with you.
I fear to write to be free,
less slave and I doubt without believing
in words, in speeches
and I emerge like the lichen with the roots
of the willows in calm.

I'm afraid to breathe if I'm awake
if I leave the windows open
from my home to leak a piece of heaven,
to see the remoteness without a border
that stretches out
where the twisting of the earth ends
and infinity begins.

I am afraid of the avenues,
to the footsteps that are not of the pilgrim,
to discover the walls and the barbed wire fences
that injustice builds, as the children sprout
in third countries, those children who go astray
losing more than naivety,
without a piece of bread; those children without faces,
as barefoot as their souls are naked
as they grow among the thorns
and disappear among the weeds of the peoples.

With metaphor.

With the parable of your lips
I write poems,
I thresh out assonances
and with the synalepha of your being
I descend and climb
seeking in your beauty
the forbidden between two.

Outlining what you have
we dress on the outside
and we hide everywhere,
like two naughty children
without anyone understanding
what I carry inside,
what I feel for you,
trying to plagiarize the passion
as those who love do
without asking permission,
without justifying forgiveness or sin.

I am not...

I am not of the earth,
I have no roof,
nor holes to bury
what I have;
I am not a tree, I am not a seed,
I am from up there,
if I go far away if I am very close.

I am a sailor without a port,
cloud traveling adrift,
sailboat without anchor and without sails,
shipwrecked, a slave and not a soldier.

I am not of the earth,
my sons Dhazin and my Alfredillo,
the wind tells me so
with its tremulous rhymes,
the sound of my footsteps exclaim it
through the shortcuts of silence
and I am only that in time:
trope, metaphor, empty amphora,
man, an arrow that gets lost
as my hands get lost
when they flutter for you,
after loving you so much...

The socialists of Latin America
are a gang of corrupt people
with their sharp fangs
thirsty for power and wealth.

They are an organized mafia
that plunder our nations
who enslave our countries
in the name of foreign ideologies
are dangerous specimens,
the lime of our nations,
those who mock our misfortune,
our ignorance, our poverty,
the navel of underdevelopment,
of the fear provoked by injustice,
hunger and misery.

And I who write verses,
odes that rhyme with the freedom
to love, to think, and to doubt,
and I am not a projectile, nor a grenade.
and I denounce the art of manipulation
the profession of those who control us,
if we fast, if we do not believe, if we think differently,
whether we live asleep or awake,
if we yearn for democracy, not fictitious democracy,
whether we disagree with the capitalists,
with the communists, with the anarchists,
with the sects, with the fanatics,
if we respect the martyrs,
to the heroes and not to any god,

nor to a chosen One, nor to a Messiah,
because we are minus or a plus,
a zero, -perhaps,- in the arena of the universe
or maybe more than a people
in the past, in the present, and in the future.

Longing.

Longing for broken glass
at the edges of the heart,
homesickness of the downpour with its notes
reviving sadness and happiness
in the most inhospitable exile.

And I miss you, loneliness,
-you don't understand it.-
because your language embraces,
descends and falls without the explanation
of the resounding, of the everyday.

Today boredom has a new countenance
at the window without your face, love,
while the sharpness of the years cuts mysterious
with the softness of yesterday,
and in every bend where memories accumulate
like sinister hills,
the corpses cursed by love
and by hatred, they forgot to bury them
in the ruins of our world.

Brief Ode to Latin America.

They flee from hunger, corruption,
of inequalities, of organized mafias,
of the guerrillas,
drug traffickers and terrorists,
because of so many parasitic governments
and so many socialist dictatorships
that exist in their countries condemned
by infamy, by poverty,
misery and underdevelopment:
Latin America's womb.

They flee their nations like wet backs or not,
like trembling shadows furrowing valleys,
mountains, rivers, deserts,
swamps, seas, lakes, hells,
tiny paradises that end in the nightmare
of living in third worlds.
And they are like a people without a voice,
without a throat, a lost people,
a people without a vertebra,
a people who are shipwrecked again and again
and do not emerge afloat through the centuries,
a people controlled by bloody revolutions,
by treacherous politicians,
by the art of ignorance,
by a handful of communists,
by the curse of believing in so many gods,
in so many saints and in despotic prophets.

Latin America,
you are a people buried in history

by a bloody conquest
that is still hard to remember with the suffering
of our ancestors, outraged, enslaved, raped,
annihilated and plundered
to where the brevity of life ends
and begin the immensity of pain and death...

Between the sword and the wall.

Between the sword and the wall,
without wall and without a sword,
without love, without hate,
forgotten and indifferent,
tortured, persecuted,
imprisoned and misunderstood,
I fall into the emptiness
without reaching the bottom
of everything, of nothing.

And madness is the antidote
of the cruelest suffering
that I feel for you, humanity...

Motives. -IV-

I hang my clothes
on the clotheslines in my room
and I lose myself in the verses
of other bards who make me dream,
to think, to doubt, not to fear
and without their understanding
the reason of lyricism,
sometimes, -only sometimes-
I denounce with the unchained prose of silence
the sinister darkness
that the history of the peoples
knew how to hide with its pathetic gods,
with its tyrannical prophets
and with their intelligent demons,
mocking me,
of you, of all...

With the cascade
of your laughter
I rehearse the notes
that intones
the hymn of love
and when our kisses
rumble in the darkness
of our room
we discover
what love is made of.

Of insomnia.

-I-

It is winter,
it dawned gray in the city
that lends me its roads
to extend my exile
in the desert of Las Vegas
and today there will be no moaning for you
the rain that falls from the sky
quenching the thirst of the stones
in these infertile lands
where the freedom to dream
and to live is not forbidden
by no socialist dictatorship.

-II-

Stop bending your neck
swan of melancholy,
that even if you have big wings
and fly high, you do not escape
from the imagination that my hands feel.

-III-

A spider stopped weaving
the loneliness on the ceiling of my skull
during my sleepless nights
and the cheerful ashtrays of the corner bar
no longer speak of the unfinished stories
of anonymous alcoholics
censored by repressed whores,

by erotic fantasies
who fear to enjoy the true phallus
of desire and not of love.

My island.

My island remained somewhere in my memories:
blue, green, and yellow,
white foam, white sky
and in its sea, she sails lonely,
half-lizard, half maiden,
ashen of the Caribbean, pouting and cheerful
and before it was the pearl of the Americas
and today it is mourned by a dictatorship
for more than six decades of hunger,
of poverty and injustice.
And they plunder my Cuba,
a handful of evildoers outrage you,
rape you, just because in the name
of the swindle of socialism
and of a pathetic revolution.

And you will continue to be my island, -forever-
far from my heart or close to my soul,
virgin bride, lover, woman,
lips smiling on the horizon,
full of corals, of reefs,
of mountains, of plains, of hillsides,
of palm trees; clear as the ocean waters
that dress your shores,
that sprinkle your geography with saltpeter
and you flutter like a wounded bird
that refuses to die before
and after each dawn.

Damned.

Condemned to be slaves,
to lose our identity,
to live from day to day,
fearful of the hand that feeds us
with the sacrifice of sweat
in the forge of the worker.

Condemned to know how to lie,
not to tell the truth
because justice is a golden thread
woven by the powerful
when they govern, when they impose
war and peace,
democracy, dictatorships,
poverty and prosperity.

Fearful of being or not being,
of losing everything, of having a little too much,
of being cursed forever
by the gods, by the demons, and by the prophets
that they have invented to control us better,
every day, every year, century after century.

Sentenced to die
from the first breath of life
by the ordeal of time,
trapped in our bodies
that will detonate from within
with the ethereal sound of death,
trapped in the immense cage of this planet,
unable to jump into the abyss

of the universe and be free forever.

But to have identity is to think,
is to rebel, is to doubt and not to believe,
is to exist struggling to disappear sooner or later,
 until the day that science and technology will discover
that immortality not only belongs to the gods,
to angels and demons,
but also to men.

January.

January.
Snow in the Nevada desert
and the mourning ostracism
misses the Ladies in White who still fight for freedom
of my oppressed, outraged, and violated Cuba,
by the longest dictatorship
that exists in Latin America:
The Castro dictatorship.

And my verse that does not rhyme with anything,
-disabled in a wheelchair, -
seeks among other forms your image,
the love I have not had,
the hatred that deflates like a balloon,
and although in politics sometimes my poems,
 -broken by uncertainty,-
they mix love and hate,
and not those sublime and sinister things
that men invent
in times of peace and war.

September.

September reminds me
that I was young once,
that today I am older
in the mirror, in the clock melting
its hands every hour
and in spite of everything I'm intoxicated
by the pauper yearning
of the withered leaves of the trees
when they fall off in autumn,
-finally free-
because of the breeze, the sun, and the dust
that lengthens the monotony of my hands.

September accommodates the weeks
in my ribs, I watch it go by
like the water of a downpour
trickling through the streets
of this city asphalting our lives,
like the night that asphalts everything
with its perpetual darkness
between your eyes and mine.

It turns out.

It is impossible to forget you,
to untie the knots of memory
at the crossroads of the years
without drinking the toxin of time
to poison oneself more on the outside
than inside in the game of living
and dying, of sowing evil,
of fertilizing love when there is no love
and to be colorless as the oxygen we breathe,
like the water that falls from the sky,
like the space that monopolizes everything,
fearing to doubt for believing too much,
while no one will change for the better
the history of mankind,
nor the end of our world
slowly dying out.

And this is living...?

Green fruits,
ripe fruits,
rotten fruits,
spring, summer,
autumn and winter,
north, south,
east and west,
love, hate,
rich and poor,
misery, opulence,
war and peace,
god and the devil,
light and darkness,
democracy and dictatorships,
socialism and capitalism,
truth and lies,
to be born, to grow,
multiply and die...
And this is living?

When will...?

When will it stop
to be summer
in the month of November
and the spring will stop bleeding
in winter
so that love does not wither
after we fall
and we get up,
even if it costs the existence
to spread love without love,
to gather the fruits of hatred
and divide them into unequal parts
in the enormous prison of this planet?
we did not try again
when our love melted
and our hearts
ceased to be the drums of joy.

Pride was stronger,
the incomprehension of feeling,
vanity and indifference than those things we gave each other,
pure and crystalline, light and very deep,
overflowing the cascades of desire.

After all,
the years rained in memories
like ephemeris made of paper
and what was left in the bonfires of the past
will never be translated by oblivion
in my verses, nor in my prose,
but they will remain there,

175

tamped on the plain of our history,
stretched out in eternal dawns
when we had not tired
of loving each other so many times
in the huge subject of life.

I love, I cry...

I love, I cry,
I am not a coward
and if I was, if I am,
who cares
the symphony of your eyes,
your accidental sensuality
and the epic of your lips
of sponges and not of rocks?

I scream, I sing,
I play the guitar of your body
and I love the silence if I cry, if I roar,
if I denounce for living
to death and not to the invention
of sin that they invented
to control us better.

The darkness...

Darkness germinates in tenderness
as your thighs ripen
pressed and precise
in the stems of your legs
and in the petals of your sex, woman.

And I, without being the elf of passion,
I seek your softness:
warm season and candle
in the not paradisiacal garden
of those who love each other
and if I am not crazy
in the reality that consumes us,
I pretend the sanity
of the worst of poets,
and I write verses
that tastes like you...

I wanted...

I wanted to tell you everything,
to give you everything, -or almost everything-, -
and not in fragile kisses-.
that dissipate in the morning,
in the wings of night butterflies.
And I knew that your anatomy
is the lyricism that fits
in the song of nature
and after so much and so little
I tried to discover you with what is leftover
to my manhood on the relief of your skin,
with half the moon in your eyes,
with the night sheltering us from fear
and I understood that loving you is not so simple,
that it takes more than a soul
and a heart in the motive
that spills the sweetness of your being
anywhere in the universe.

One more day...

One more day death parades
with the edge of time aborting genocides,
asthmatic guerrillas,
bloody revolutions,
socialist dictatorships,
corrupt regimes
and the gods of the peoples continue to mock our misfortune
playing at being eternal,
condemning us with the justification
of sin, of disobedience
and the prophets of always,
tyrants and masters of manipulation
still, give us hate to drink,
fanaticism and not the hemlock that ends our eternal curse.

And history does not change with hunger,
with the misery, with the inequalities
that accumulate in the sinkhole of Latin America,
but it does change with technology;
the rich become more powerful
and on the weight of the stones in the desert of exile,
loneliness and melancholy
is the music of light tones,
while the good peoples cease to love
because love is only that:
oblivion, absence, renunciation,
past, present, and future.

When I am left.

When I run out of light
I will not be afraid
because everything will not end there,
where death invented
a pit in the bosom of the earth
to turn our bones into dust.

We will no longer be in the space
where neurons connect,
tissues and bones
and the blood runs in tubular labyrinths;
we will be less than silent,
atoms that are concatenated with the infinite
and in the eternal night with the springs of stars,
of planets, of galaxies,
where everything that ends one day,
transforms and never fades away.

In the streets...

In the streets of pain
they are impartial shadows
and at the crossroads of misfortune,
wet backs, faces without names,
an endangered species,
citizens of third worlds:
the peoples of Latin America
fleeing hunger and hardship,
because of corrupt regimes
and communist dictatorships
that destroy and plunder their countries.
And there are thousands and millions of human beings
who seek the roads to the North
and they cross seas, rivers, lakes, mountains, hills, plains
swamps, deserts, and jungles,
with the language of fear in their expressions,
of despair in their eyes,
with courage in their souls,
light of baggage,
naked inside and out,
to find in a strange land,
there, in the distance, the American dream:
bread on the table,
a roof and a bed, an honest job,
justice and equality, in a faraway country,
where no one has yet murdered
freedom and democracy.

I try to leave you...

I try to leave you,
divorce you,
not to do without your essence
in the icy mornings,
on the hottest days,
hanging indifference
on the altars of ostracism.

I would renounce your name,
the spell that springs
through the pores of your being,
the art you give away
without asking for anything,
though you are so much and I am so little
that writing you on the walls,
on the sheets, on the blackboards,
on the monitor of a computer,
on the screen of a tablet,
of a cell phone, you will never cease to be poetry
in my hands, in my breath
and in the respected hymn of the peoples.

If death...

If death tastes like to eternity,
life is a miserable quota of existence.

If the fertile has plenty of martyrdom,
what is sterile is embraced by melancholy
like the all-encompassing desert
in its sea of rocks, sands
and of stones filled with the echoes of other times,
echoes of infinity.

If I do not sing and eat flowers,
if I am wounded by thorny stalks,
I ride naked with the imagination
of the new moon.

If in my madness of loving you
I throw myself on the precipice of your body,
I am reborn again and again
every morning like a phoenix,
contemplating the beauty of your face, woman.

Who to blame...?

Whom to blame for the imbalance
and misfortune of mankind?
god, the devil, the homeless who walk the streets?
without asking permission for being freer than you,
mocking the contemporary slaves,
mocking the drug traffickers, the mafias,
of ideologies, of fanaticism,
of the suicides, of the laws, of the prostitutes
and of those who buy their meat?

Whom to blame?
To the dim light, to the perpetual darkness,
the lie, the truth,
the laconism of every nightfall?
The colors that do not match,
the liquids that do not mix
in the sewers of nations?

Whom to blame?
The monists, the dualists,
the cruelty of nature,
the heterosexual, the homosexual,
the imposition of death,
the tremulous eyelid that hides the windows of the soul,
Nietzsche sweeping with his leaden mustache
the streets of philosophy?

Whom to blame: our parents, our brothers, and sisters,
our children in the loop of existence,
the first stone that built our world,

185

the mystery that never was,
the first drop of water that formed the oceans,
to Homo sapiens, to Homo erectus,
to Charles Darwin, to Karl Marx,
Hitler, Lenin, the genocidal Stalin,
the Chinese criminal, Mao Zedong,
to the sublimity of love,
to the senselessness of hatred,
to so many tyrannical gods,
to so many intelligent devils,
to so many manipulative prophets,
to the myth of good and evil;
to the manipulation of truth and lies,
to war, to peace, to conflicts,
to millions of illegal migrants
who flee to the United States
like herds of beings with no future
of coexisting in their countries
subjugated by dictatorships
and corrupt regimes?

Whom to blame...?
The feathers of the birds,
the fins of the fish,
the manure, - a mixture of rotting flesh,
of urine and dust -
to time, to gravity, to weightlessness,
to the miracle, to ignorance, to erudition,
to politicians, to the work of freedom,
-parody and fiction-
to religions, to laws,
to injustice, to the sciences,
to technology, to insane asylums, to prisons,
to so many languages, to so many countries,

to so many flags, anthems, cultures,
to the borders, to the atomic missiles pointing
over our heads...

Who to blame... Do you tell me?
Who to blame...?

You mold yourself.

You mold to my flesh
like the wind in the branches,
like the music that vibrates
on the strings of a guitar,
like the clear waters
and the black waters
seeking the bends of the earth.

You mold yourself to my nakedness
designing the feeling
and you are the rain that breaks,
grows and overflows;
you mold yourself to my being
like the rotation to the waterwheel
and you enter my eyes like clarity
piercing me from the inside.

And it is the harmony of your voice,
cascading, your beauty, perfect work
and though you mold yourself to my whims
like the sunrise to the eyelids of the horizon,
you fit into my being at any hour,
with the softness of a falling petal
in the spring because you are mine.

I return discreetly.

I return discreetly and I leave,
dressed on the outside, empty on the inside,
with the resonances of nature:
pale, blue, floe
and I don't care what you think
if you love, if you curse, if you dream,
if your identity has not yet been stolen,
if you have not been manipulated
by the governments with their laws,
with their schools, with their universities
and with so many socialist teachers
lovers of capitalism,
of the propaganda of the powerful
and more than one people explode
with the nightmares of underdevelopment
that do not fit in the cabinets of history,
of the poverty of all,
without stabbing a dagger in the back
to the enemies of humanity
in the jungle of survival,
trying to get afloat,
shipwrecked in the attempt to be free.

I was left...

I was left without my homeland
when I tried to break the chains:
free from hunger, from poverty,
and from the injustice programmed
by the worst and longest dictatorship
that exists in Latin America
that took over my nation,
in the name of the socialism scam,
enslaving millions of Cubans.

And sometimes it is harder than the twelve years
I spent in the political prison, the exile:
living on foreign soil, where you walk,
you eat and breathe, you speak another language,
you learn new customs,
acclimatize yourself to everything,
with the face of indifference and loneliness
digging deep into the pockets of the soul,
but free, yes, free, with the democracy of other peoples,
which is now mine:
bread on the table, good wine, and justice.

And though time and distance
bury everything, all things pass away,
nothing remains in memory as a seed,
nor in the history of a country that is not mine,
which I admire and respect,
where love blossoms and something more,
far from the place where my roots were cut
and I began to grow like a fern
in the shadows of ostracism.

Today...

Today
I'm not in such a hurry
to love you more than yesterday,
in a place where passion
is entrenched
in the cliffs of hate
and imagination flies away
from the prison of my body,
because at any time
you give me everything,
natural, without make-up,
drop by drop,
filling the emptiness of this man
who is for you a child,
a young man and an old man.

I move away from the worldly noise
and I seek in the stillness the notes
that innovate those who love each other
in the shortest morning
and in the subtle night.

And that melody is fragile fluttering,
whispering of the air, drops ringing
in the blinds of the heart.

Distant from all, -not from you,-
poetry, I think of her,
and of solid steel, concrete
and fragile blade,
I write verses to the first love
who took away my innocence
with her tender hands and her beautiful face.

Why see you again...

Why see you again,
why if I don't miss you
and if I miss you
we will repeat the same
in the attempt to love each other
surrounded by thorns
without the scent of flowers,
besieged by the leafiness
of the shadows of the living,
without thinking of a paradise,
but in the hell
of your world and mine.

I invite you.

I invite you to live to suffer,
to smile with sadness,
to measure pain, not happiness,
to not be afraid,
to not believe, to doubt,
to breathe the freedom of being
with the identity not prostituted
by governments,
to conquer love,
to defeat hatred
on the balconies of melancholy;
I invite you to denounce the evil
that like a wound
does not heal outside or inside
of the vestiges of humanity.
I invite you to sell nice and cheap
those things that have no value
 in the market of life.

What I dreamed of so much.

My best poem will not be for me,
I will not write it to eternity,
without feeling spite for death,
but for the contempt of the tyrannical god
invented by men.

My last poem will emigrate in search
of new borders
and will reclaim from freedom
what I was not, what I will be,
and like the keel of a sailboat
sailing the seas,
it will raise its sails in the space
where the particles of my bones
will mingle with the earth,
with water and fire,
without denying existence
what I dreamed of so much.

Silent song.

When the daring and flirtatious moon
is an orange hanging up there,
without the earth biting its other half,
the sailor sets sail unhurriedly in his boat,
in love with the waves
to fish the virginity of the sea
with nylon and bait tied to the hook.

And he does not fish for flowers, nor birds,
nor fruits, nor palm trees,
he fishes the dreams of being a sailor:
free and landless man.

And at night his sky is as wide
as the current that carries him adrift,
sailing aimlessly,
tuning the flashes
of the stars in the distance,
with a silent song that listens
moody and joyful:

"It is the music of foam and saltpeter
the sublime notes that sway in the wind,
yesterday, today, and tomorrow,
even though they dissipate
in the infinite with the brevity
of life and death..."

Why live...?

Why live-trapped
in the immense cage of this world
made to our measure
in the infinity of the universe,
of emptiness, of nothingness,
in the most terrifying of mysteries?

To live for what, you tell me:
to be born, to grow, to multiply and to die,
condemned in our bodies
without anyone having asked our permission
to bring us to this planet of death,
controlled by evil, by greed,
by wars and conflicts,
by a tyrannical god and an intelligent demon:
-science fiction, mediocre literature.-

You tell me: live for what?
to repeat what has been repeatable for centuries:
rich and poor, misery and opulence,
social inequalities
multiplying with the unsustainable numbers of injustice;
bad governments, parasitic politicians,
fictitious democracy,
and capitalists so hungry for power and wealth,
ready to exploit and destroy everything.

I will not undress you.

I will not undress you
as the breeze undresses
to the daisies,
to the ferns in the shadows,
to the calm lilies,
to the flower petals,
to its thorns, to the stems.

I will leave you like the rain leaves the grass,
to the leaves of the trees,
to the land, to the rivers,
to the springs,
to the rhyme of the drops of water
ringing love notes
on the ground,
on the walls, on the rooftops
and you will not forget that I too
I bled silently for you

We ran out of everything.

It's all over as the last summer's rainstorm
on the ruins of the past -not of the present.

We ended the pregnancy of the feeling,
without calculating depth and surface
of love and hate, because the trousseau of youth
change clothes so many times,
oblivious to the fashion of existence.

After giving us so much,
to share the lights of passion eternal mornings
and so many sunsets exploding in our bodies,
the misunderstanding raised the anchor
and I sailed in the sea of love without goodbyes.

And we ended up like this
how the waters disappear
of the rivers in the oasis of affection,
how the dew evaporates
before dawn,
like a kiss that separates from the lips
break what they measure
lovers with their absence.

I caress you.

I caress you without my hands,
with a borrowed heart
that beats in my chest
and with the other half of my being
I am a minus and a plus
in the pupils of desire
and straining like the first time
when I made love to you
where the night lends us
its forbidden intimacy,
the sunset is not a farewell
nor the dawn a break
of being or not being.

Thinking of you.

Thinking of you
I tied the laces
of fantasy
and untied the melancholy
buried in the present
to forget you
because your memories lacerate
accumulating in the heart
like useless shadows
in the dustbin of time.

Of realities. –III–

*You defeat me
without weapons,
without metaphors,
without rhetoric,
without speeches,
when in the word
of silence
you turn off the light
and the darkness
of our bedroom
lends itself
to take off our clothes
and overcome the fear
of loving each other again
looking at us from the inside.*

Your love.

Your love emerges brimming with emotions,
is allegory, parable, enigma,
thesis, hypothesis, perfect geometry,
mathematics, physics, weightlessness,
seasoning that combines
the bitter and sweet of life and death.

Your love emigrates without a homeland,
without a master, but with land,
it is current, heavy rain, lightning,
snow, the cloud that travels across continents,
it is the art of the good, a reason that tears away
from nature its origin
and it is a sadness that justifies joy,
any waste of happiness
on the altars of the heart;
your love is a tide that overflows everything,
hurricane, tropic, perpetual glaciers,
justice without scales,
fierce enemy of hatred,
faithful friend, truth, pious lie,
sparkle in any unfathomable abyss.

I am not...

I am not happy and if I were:
what would happiness do with us or without anyone?
To lend its fictitious attire,
the miserable gift of life,
the encapsulated emotion,
its strings out of tune,
broken wings of fright,
the other eye we lack,
molars not decayed, teeth useless;
it would shorten the years, tighten the skin,
we would live longer, we would stop thinking
and we would dream awake and not asleep
to land without a parachute
in the insignificant subject of existence,
without forgetting the most human language,
the hymn of the people:
"Every man for himself!"

After being born by accident
on an island condemned
by the worst socialist dictatorship
that exists in Latin America,
no one had asked me for permission to open my eyes
where the puerile game of god and the devil,
with the myth of good and evil
are our eternal misfortune,
with wars, with endless conflicts
and with all those things that fractionate
peoples ever since mankind
divided by marriage.

I would like to escape from the monotony,
like the free poem
of the poet wandering without paths
in the harsh reality of exile,
searching in the song of the night
the moody dusk
and in the eyelids of the enamored woman
the best brushstrokes of love,
but I remain trapped in my nightmares,
-which are mine and yours as well,-
without a star and without windows,
in the cracked cloisters of desire,
broken down inside and outside my being
and in every particle of my flesh,
loneliness and joy
assemble the hieroglyphics of love
and hate.

I will go...

I will go away
where the moon does not hang
in the cobwebs of the horizon,
where those who love
and those who hate do not swarm,
where the stars
turned into supernovas
explode sweeping away what is
beyond good and evil
in any world splintered
by greed, by so many religions,
by so many borders, languages,
dialects, hymns, flags,
laws and countries and continents...

Allegory. –V–

I grew up with the remnants of innocence,
in the poverty of a third world country,
without defining the shades of misery
in the panorama of my Havana,
of my city in ruins
and I ceased to be a child suckled
by the breasts of hunger,
running barefoot and almost naked through the streets,
through the dog's teeth
of the beaches in a distant place,
in my Cuba full of radiance and palm trees,
-without caring about anything, I don't know why.-
And I fell in love with the blue, gray, green, white sea,
with the sun swaying among the clouds,
with the stampede of sunset and sunrise
and every comet that flew fearlessly
in the sky of my childhood,
over the rooftops of the buildings
of my surrealist city, turned into a labyrinth,
in death traps, in abysses of death,
have stories, fleeting dreams,
utopias that flutter in the past,
where other infants like the child I was,
when they are teenagers will search like me,
beyond the walls of the ocean
that besieges our island,
-Cinderella of the Caribbean,-
the freedom we lost
without a piece of bread on the table...

It occurs to me.

It occurs to me to think that I no longer love you,
that after so many decades
of tying the cords of desire
our feet are not the same,
neither are our hands,
nor my phallus nor your sex entertained
in the hanging gardens of your thighs,
where your beauty has been squeezed
slowly between my fingers
like circus tents
for caressing you so much and if I look at what is left
of me and you in the mirror of time:
what did I discover above
or below the relief of our skin?
Cracks that pierce the continent of the faces?
A steppe in the scaffolding
of bones, of what we once were:
imitation of an oasis,
 penguins on a glacier
trying to take a flight?

Take my sleep away love.

Take my sleep away love,
I want to wake up with you,
this lonely heart
hunter of your passion
needs to be filled with your kisses,
to overflow with your caresses
when without clothes the two of us
make peace and war
and of a miniature hell,
the paradise that was denied
to those who loved each other
for the first time.

Let me undress you slowly and in a hurry,
to capture with your intimacy
in the brevity of the minutes
of pleasure, glory and madness
that unites a man and a woman.

I love you.

I love you drop by drop,
of hat and umbrella,
from downpour and drizzle,
from sunshine to dew, from sea to river,
from summer and winter,
from spring and waterfall,
of firmament and space,
of abyss and infinity in miniature,
of golden sun and silver moon,
of plain and mountain,
of immense sea and mighty river,
of night and sunrise,
of rhythm and poetry,
of freedom and justice,
of tree and fruit,
of earth, of root and seed,
of man and woman, of love and hate
because you are and will be the other part
of my cells, of my particles,
woman, my beloved.

Joyful by your side.

Love,
I would like to be with you,
in the dark, with the light of your gaze,
to feel your porcelain nudity
turned into a work of art between my hands;
to perceive your beauty complicating
the emotions of this man
who stopped being a child in love
of those things of yours that do not fit
in my atoms.

And without you knowing what I feel
I'm afraid to love you
and then lose you
because life is short
and time is so long
that tomorrow we won't be the same
on the map of our bodies,
and like a wandering being
along the paths of the years,
I'll pretend to be old,
to be joyful by your side.

Woman,
better than you, no one,
worse than you, me,
-man, animal.-

Poetry knows it,
music, art,
my piece of heaven,
the complicity of god
and of the demons
believing themselves powerful
because they are eternal,
the true tyrants
of humanity.

Impossible love.

I search among my verses
for your silhouette,
the beauty you squander,
the love I have not had,
the longing that in the spring
is stronger than autumn,
than the myth of hope
and the lie of the miracle,
and without you noticing
how much I miss you
in the improvised ostracism
of men without a homeland,
I die slowly for you,
and I will never stop loving you in the distance,
with the fierceness of indifference
because our love is and will be
an impossible love.

Of things.

I

*You don't need to be a scholar or an intellectual
to understand the scenario of history.
And which history...?*

II

*We are programmed to be born,
grow, multiply and die
in the gigantic prison of our planet,
without understanding, -for the moment-
that immortality is a pseudonym
of science and technology,
that what the peoples forge for centuries,
with their tyrannical gods
with their intelligent demons
and with their manipulative prophets,
is the epitome of fallacy.*

III

*To commit suicide is not for cowards,
cowards are those who accept
the imposition to exist,
condemned to death from the first day
who breathe without identity.*

VI

*To be free is not to live,
to live is to be a slave to fear,*

of love and hate,
of poverty, of inequalities,
of laws, of corrupt governments,
of dictatorships, of dynasties,
of the injustice planned
by all governments.

V

Do not forget that pain and suffering
is the panacea of the peoples
contracting marriage with humanity
to divide everything.

Thinking.

Thinking of you my agony
lends what I have to the smile,
and I don't agree with you
in the ostracism of the soul
where truth is a mimicry
that invents regimes, dictatorships,
democracy and socialism.

And it is not difficult
to balance the commiseration
on the tightrope of passion,
by elucidating the best of the Naked Maja
through the fingers of that Goya,
just as it is not difficult to elucidate
the perfect sculpture
of Michelangelo's David
in the imagination of a woman.

What will we have left tomorrow..?

What will we have left tomorrow of the air,
of the rivers, of the seas,
of the lakes and the springs;
of the seeds, of the trees,
of the birds without skies,
of the skies without clouds,
of the mountains, of the forests,
of the desert, of the plains,
of the last species in extinction?

What will we have left tomorrow
of spring, of summer,
of autumn and winter,
of the four cardinal points,
of gravity, of the moon and the sun,
of the glaciers, of another daybreak,
of the night over all,
of sunsets languishing
in the memory of the survivors
when the children no longer exist,
the birds, the roses, the war, nor the peace,
when the curse of the gods
invented by the wickedness of those who thought themselves
smarter than you and me
can no longer condemn anyone?

What will be left tomorrow of our dreams,
of those things that played
through the centuries with love and hate?
What will be left of the invention of freedom,
of the armies, of the corrupt politicians,

of the few honest men,
of nuclear weapons,
of good music, of true poetry,
of art not turned into mediocrity,
of the fertile womb of a mother,
of the poor, of the rich,
of hunger and opulence,
of the last of the lovers,
of a Romeo without Juliet,
of a José Martí dressed in black
riding his white horse,
of the cities, of the skyscrapers,
of the avenues, of the boulevards, of the meadows,
of the traffic lights, of the schools,
of the hospitals, of what they call justice,
you tell me: what will we have left tomorrow...?

It is late.

It is late,
the city sleeps,
-laughing exile, premature oasis,-
the lamps hang everywhere,
simulate fictitious suns
in the everlasting darkness,
while many wait for another day
in the heart attack of reality,
in the miniature paradise of the houses,
with their four walls,
with their roofs and windows
not to dream without eyelids,
to fill the stomachs,
and to get high on debts,
listening to the propaganda
on the wheel of capitalism.

I had a spirit.

I had a spirit and I lost it
when the present withered away,
-pasture from the past,-
I fished in the sea
and now I fish in the rivers;
I sowed in the desert
the seeds of hatred
and I began to plow love
in the sand of the beaches.

My hope that was so green
was eaten by the goats.

One day I wanted to fly and I fell into the precipice
like Icarus when his wings melted.

I tried to believe in the light and the light exploded
in my eyes like a supernova
and every year the same Santa Claus
in his happy clown outfit
appears to mourn an old year
mended ephemeris for a new year.

I have seen...

I have seen death pass by
without scythe and without black disguise,
I have seen it pass
with the identity of any face,
similar to fashion,
with her cloaks and trappings;
I have seen her with her deep throat
screaming at the sound of bullets,
of the grenades, of the missiles
and bombs destroying cities,
annihilating peoples in distant countries,
in nearby nations,
because of you, because of me,
because of everyone...

I like the glasses.

I like the glasses of your eyes,
the trifles in your eyebrows,
your eyelashes fanning the distance
in the tropic of consciousness.
I like the nighttime of your pupils
imitating the curvature of the horizon,
your violin waist
making the strings of love envious.

I like your thighs pressed and sensual
like the hanging gardens
of an absent Babylon;
to see you naked when you bathe
and when you perfume yourself with the scent
of the mysticism of the night,
while I rhyme the divinity of your flesh
with my verses broken by panic
of loving you knowing that one day
I will lose you forever.

This madness.

This madness
for your lips,
for your black hair,
for your feminine fragrance,
for your voice balancing my manhood.

This madness
for the curves that dress you
ascending and descending
through my hands,
for desiring you close,
for longing for all of you,
makes me a participant
of the suicides of love
and my ridiculous heart
so full of emotions
that overflows in your beauty,
rides like a rider
crashing without you,
after every dawn.

He is murdered so many times.

He is killed so many times
that after death he is resurrected
like those who fall and rise again
in the arms of justice,
in the clutches of corruption,
in the shrapnel of war,
in the bonanza of peace,
in the misfortune of hunger,
in the face of the disparity
of those third world countries
that many know from television,
by the newspapers, by the magazines,
through social networks, but not in the flesh.
I am not saying it, nor did I make it up,
it is sung by the minstrels of silence
with the pain of their voices crossing continents;
I hear it in the cries of millions of children
who feed on the dust and drink the dirty water,
those children who do not know a Santa Claus,
nor a toy in the worst Christmas of the poor.
And those millions of children will continue to be born
in the wombs of third worlds,
and they will die naked and barefoot,
they will not say goodbye to life,
but they will smile for the last time at death,
with their little faces peering into indifference,
because of you, because of me,
because of everyone's complicity.

What will remain...

What will be left of me,
-someday- will be less
than the miniature of the feeling,
parabola perforating the distance,
useless dust,
satire of the past,
less legend than an avalanche,
than the assaults that produce echoes
in the immensity of the full moon,
than love poems
and soulless verses,
than death not kneeling
for the most fictitious forgiveness,
-complicity of the infamy of sin.-

And all of me and you will be sunk,
-we know it, we ignore it,-
will swim over the creeks,
shall fly over the barbed wire of iniquity,
before the tempest of hatred,
without understanding the why of a before
and an after...

Again.

Again to live,
molds of faces,
born without a soul,
empty inside,
bare on the outside,
made of what:
Of flesh, of liquids?
Wrappings of skin,
of nails, of bones,
of hair, veins, and blood.

Life again:
the same loop repeating itself
through the centuries
with the myth of the gods,
of demons,
of so many manipulative prophets,
and all trapped in the enormous prison
of this planet,
sentenced to perish,
to experience love and hate,
poverty and opulence,
war and peace
and so many disparities
that protrude over the hemorrhoids
of the sphincter of the peoples.

226

I fall in love.

I fall in love
of the gray and the winter white,
allegory in my head,
and the distance
that separates
and divides,
like your love
and mine,
is migration,
anarchism,
freedom,
anatomy without vertebrae,
metastasis,
frustration and existence.

Prison.

Twelve years hit hard in the prison,
in one of the many jails
that exist in my country, Cuba,
sentenced for loving freedom,
for trying to be free and left traces so deep
that they do not fit in the soul or in the flesh,
nor in the despair when everything is lost
because of hatred.

Twelve years struck me worse
than the fictitious plagues of the four horsemen
of the Apocalypse.
Twelve years on the merry-go-round of adolescence,
at 17 years of age, condemned to perpetuity;
twelve years that cut me with the edge of injustice,
in the carnivals of rancor,
with the arrogance of the dictator, Fidel Castro.

And they were blows with tenebrous sounds
that sketched the tombstones of death
when they fall abruptly burying
in oblivion to the living,
with no one to hear their grieving voices,
nor the anonymous suffering over the remains of those
who manage to survive against all hope.

Twelve years accumulated cracks in the skin,
webs of hunger in the sphincters
of the rebellion of the best men,
of the patriots, of the brave,
of those planted, in hunger strikes,

drawing on the ribs
the exemplary tortures
and the repression planned
by the worst and longest socialist dictatorship
in Latin America.

I see them being born...

I see them being born, stoic,
with the identity stolen from them
the governments, the dictatorships,
in the name of democracy and socialism.

I see them born indifferent
because of their parents,
because of so many religions,
because of illiteracy,
of indoctrination in schools,
of social injustice
and they grow like ferns
in the shadows of mediocrity,
addicted to the ignorance, to the propaganda,
to bottled commercials,
to drugs, to the imposition of fashion,
slaves to the fear produced the laws,
the politicians, the democracy,
the dictatorships and the echoes of being born,
growing, multiplying, and dying
in the immense cage of our world.

My adolescence.

My adolescence broke like a wave,
before and after a storm;
it crashed against the reefs
of lawlessness and swept my innocence
on the cliffs of hatred,
discovering behind the walls,
the fences and bars of the political prison
the shocks of living,
of loving and dreaming,
that like the undertow of destiny,
fall on the shoulders of men
to turn them into more beasts
or more human.

Elegy.

Mario limps on his right leg,
walks like a wobbling clock
with a poetic, surreal ticking...

He is a guy who sprouted in a faraway place,
in a land that suffers from corruption,
with conflicts that destroy his people
like an incurable disease.

And fleeing from hunger
and the injustice that exists in his homeland,
he crossed nations, mountains, jungles,
weeds, rivers, hills,
the invisible and imposing walls of the borders
that divide our continent.
And he arrived full of hope,
with the desire to live better,
without changing its language,
his culture, nor his religion,
anonymous like the shadows
of the wetbacks in the USA,
looking for the American dream,
to forget the misfortune
and the eternal curse that our peoples
in Latin America suffer,
condemned by their rotten governments
by the revolutions of the wicked
and by so many socialist dictatorships.

She died...

"To Margiolis."

She died of love,
burned her child's soul,
her skin and her naked heart
in the chimera of her adolescence,
in her early womanhood.
She died without cowardice,
like a girl who was snatched away
what was left of her innocence,
without understanding the game of those who
who are passionate about the desire for a female.

And everyone knew what happened to her
one day in August
when sadness was blacker
than the stones in the quarries of the night
of the eyes that sleep awake contemplating the decay.

She died of love, so alone,
abandoned by life,
yes, of love she died in the bonfire
that unleashes madness,
because of those who sought her
to possess her for an instant,
because she gave herself easily,
without saying goodbye to the intense fervor
when for love one surrenders all,
being the bait on the hook
of men's fieriness.

And she danced, walked, and smiled

like a creature who did not calculate her steps,
without putting a price on the pleasure that blossomed
in the beauty of her youth.

She lived breathing the happiness of all,
in the surrealist hell where she was born,
tearing down the walls of poverty,
of sadness, of indifference, of loneliness,
and the fear of growing up in a third-world country.

And she, without saying goodbye to anyone,
she committed suicide in the carnival of the fire
that devoured her existence,
she committed suicide for the little that life had given her
in the terrifying silence of inequalities,
because of the incomprehension of feeling,
of the absence of his parents, of his brothers,
of her friends, of the men who loved
her Creole guitar curves,
of mulatto without history in the Caribbean,
in a country forgotten by time.

Your anatomy.

Your anatomy has luxurious lace,
seasoning of the tropics,
agonizing anguish, inner musicality,
paradise of two, the inferno of all.

The molds of your figure are the riddles
that glimpse perfection
in the cartography of the world
and in the latitudes that defy the gravity of being
and the weightlessness of not being,
magnifies love, truth,
vanity and pride,
produces wars, conflicts,
temporary peace, fleeting justice,
and what concatenates
the sentiment of the multitudes.

Your beauty of parchment,
of clay sculpture, of Lladró, of flesh and fabrics,
is a delicate petal,
dew, rainbow, mud, and seed,
tornado and hurricane,
it has furrows, trenches,
caverns, sinkholes, paths, horizons, borders
horizons, borders,
walls and balusters
and everything that proliferates nourishes it
with darkness and light,
multiplies and destroys,
for being in time dust, ashes and dung.

I doubt I do not believe.

I doubt I do not believe
and I do not imitate hatred,
although it is fashionable
and love is a scarecrow.

I give when I have little
and if I have, I don't give a charity.
I give more when I have no bread to spare,
the wine on the table, some dishes,
the mute cutlery
and a few coins in my pockets,
without being like the hypocrites
because I do not compose
the mediocrity of their mercy,
nor do I feel pity for anyone
in the dumpster of the masses,
of those who feel they have more shoulders,
arms and backs,
powerful without having a light of their own.

I wish I could give you...

I wish I could give you
something new,
that is not
the plagiarism of love
or hate,
something that is not made
by a mythical god
nor by the echoes
of the imagination
of so many demons,
but that is impossible,
like denouncing my fingers
fluttering in the starry sky
that exists under your skin.

Poem to Nicolás Guillén.

Nicolás Guillén I no longer have in exile
a dictatorship to suffer because of the Castro's mafia of
revolutionaries
plundering and destroying my country
for more than sixty years
and enslaving millions of Cubans
with the imposition of hunger,
of poverty, of injustice,
indoctrination in the schools
and with the manipulation of the ideology of lies.

Now I have Nicolás Guillen,
-and today I can write it down in these verses
so that you may hear it in the grave, -
I have what millions of Cubans do not have
trapped in the enormous field
of passive extermination of our island prison:
I have in my exile an exemplary democracy
in the American nation,
I have a dream that came true
and a blue and white hope;
I have Nicolás Guillén, justice,
and the prosperity of this people,
which ironically is not the country where I was born,
but Nicolás Guillén, I have what I had to have:
an honest job, a humble family,
a house where my children are growing up,
two cars that I bought with the sweat of my brow,
a table that my people don't have there
with daily bread, with seafood,
with beef and good wine.

That and much more, Nicolás Guillen,
is what I have in this strange land,
just like those millions of Cubans
who were able to flee our oppressed homeland.

I have Nicolás Guillén what I never had in my motherland
because of the Castro dictatorship
with their fictitious revolution and the socialism swindle.
Today I have what I had to have,
Nicolás Guillén, what I did not have in my Cuba:
Freedom!

Who will take away from me...

Who will snatch your beauty from my eyes?
from my burnt memories,
the reminiscences of love accumulating
in the grottoes of past and present,
in the theme of living facing the sun
and not with my back to reality?
It seems that everything is an entourage
in the outburst of nature,
with its programmed seasons
in the wheel of our planet.

Your fault, -everyone's fault,-
curse climbing skulls,
puerile sins capsizing,
regrets reaping
evil, hatred, and injustice.

And always in your womb the same:
earth, rain, dew, dew, fertilizer, seeds
that will sprout like the teeth of the peoples,
like fruits that will ripen,
like the stalks that will lengthen,
like the strong and fragile trunks,
under the squall of the years
in the lintels of the centuries.

After all or nothing,
who will be the ones to tie
the invisible knot of death,
those who will uncover the pressure cookers

with the leftovers of fallacy,
of ignominy, of ignorance,
of manipulation, and immorality
in the dregs of humanity?

What I have left behind,
swells with the reminiscences
of love and hate
and are the work paved
by suffering and misery:
the anguish of the people,
bubbles that do not break
with the nails of wickedness
and of the greed of the capitalists
and socialists,
after so much,
after nothing.

I tried...

I tried to lift the anchor,
to flee without horizon,
to understand the ocean merging
with the firmament
and I didn't become a half-moon,
stranded in the hospitable
desert of my exile,
in a distant country,
in the land of all,
loving solitude, silence,
indifference, cowardice
and despising tyrants.

Of concerns.

I

I loved you like the fork on the table
likes to dig into the food
and feast in the mouth.

II

If tomorrow I die I will miss you
and in the aphonia of the shadows
I'll be waiting for you, love.

III
In the curvature of your lips I get lost
to find in your eyes
the doors that open the paradise of love.

IV

To fall in love you have to give everything,
without asking for an explanation,
-You know it better than me, woman.-

V
When our kisses
raise their wings and unite our bodies,
they are fireflies that illuminate
the darkness of two
in the anonymity of life's brevity.

With the debt.

245

With the debt of love
and the interest of the flesh
you turned me into an owl,
sleeping in your nakedness
and hunting like a tiger
without teeth and nails
those things of yours
that bring back inspiration and art,
forgetting the suicides
who invent governments.

And the day dances among the beaters,
among the men who are, -who were,-
because injustice is a golden thread
woven by the powerful
to make us prisoners of fear.

245

That mulatto female.

That mulatto female lived in hunger,
in misery, without freedom,
suffering everything in nothingness,
in the nightmare of sleeping
without dreaming of a better tomorrow,
with the fear that Cuban "jineteras"
selling their flesh,
their identity and sentiment
to feed the revolution
and the swindle of socialism
of the Castro's mafia;
that Cuban mulatto female
gave herself to the Canadian and European tourists,
for a pair of panties, for bras,
for toilet paper, for panties,
for clothes, for a plate of food,
for a few beers and a few shots of run,
for listening to other music
in the hell of their island called paradise
that would take her away from the sad reality
of being born in a third world country
backward in time
and forgotten in history,
with the worst and longest dictatorship
in Latin America.

The day
they assassinate poetry
the last poet
will not write verses,
he will throw poisoned arrows
with the strings of his lyre
at the vulgar ones
who think they are artists,
musicians, ballads,
and to those who are accomplices of mediocrity
and in the impurity of culture
will ferment hate and love,
mingling like dirty waters
and the limpid waters
that drain silently
between the crevices of the rocks
and through the earth to where
the bottom of life and death
is an abyss.

*The guitar vibrates
with its gloomy notes
in the night of all nights.*

*Someone makes love
to its vibrating strings,
in love with its contours
like a daring female:
Is the musician of solitude,
an anonymous ghost
and I who am in the distance
the ear that feels those melodies
penetrate my senses,
I suffer and I weep in a corner
where no one hears the sound
of my tears falling
because of a woman.*

I shelter
in your breasts,
I descend into your hair
and I walk through your meadows,
through your plains,
naked and unhurried,
fearing nothing,
leaping over walls and borders,
where the suns of your eyes
do not deny their light
after loving you.

Words, only words...

Words, only words
that weave in the threads of time
words that like links
bind chains and enslave
with truth and lies.

Words that in the air
fabricate in the echo of the peoples
their mythical gods and demons
and their tyrannical prophets;
words that sentence
justifying cruelty, faith,
light and darkness,
the fear that produces ignorance,
the laws, the governments,
injustice, democracy,
socialist dictatorships,
capitalism, the subjugation of the proletariat,
the speeches of politicians
and fashion propaganda.

Words, only words
that ignites the gunpowder of war,
that invent frontiers, armies,
science, technology,
prisons, concentration camps,
walls, tortures, electric chairs,
calvaries, hemlocks, insane asylums,
armies, mercenaries,
narcos, drug addicts, guerrillas, bombs, missiles,

250

denunciations, censorship in social networks,
mafias, inequalities, third world nations,
genocides who were and are presidents,
poverty, opulence, fictitious miracles
that canonize fanaticism,
state terrorism, abortions,
the Covid-19, crimes against humanity.

Words, only words that produce judges,
lawyers, pimps, prostitutes,
diplomats, corruption,
ideologies, novels, poetry, art without art
and that in the beginning and in the end
of existence are and will be words...

I want you...

I want you like fire wants water,
like hate to love,
as lightning to the tree,
as the cloud to the earth,
as the time to life,
as evil to good,
as the storm to the ocean,
as light to darkness,
as the war to peace,
as the labyrinth to the gates,
as the bird to the cage,
as death to life,
as truth to lies,
as the worker to capitalism,
as opulence to misery,
as corruption to justice,
as the hook to the fish,
as the hunter to his prey,
as science to religion,
as ignorance to the masses,
as politicians to speeches,
as glaciers to the tropics,
as a people to a tyrant,
as censorship to those who think,
as art to mediocrity,
as youth to old age,
as democracy to socialism,
as the soldier to the enemy,
as chains to slaves,
as happiness to sadness
and pain to joy,
because desire is less than that and nothing more: desire.

The hours arrive.

The hours arrive, they multiply in years,
in decades and time, -synonymous with death,-
begins to fit its pins
in the bones, in the organs, in the flesh, in the skin
and life starts to sway
on the tightrope over the precipice
of loneliness, of broken melancholy of fright,
in the inevitability of the sinister,
and in the silence of the theory of being,
of not being, you discover that God and the Demon
are a swindle, that the so-called prophets
already turned to dust
continue to control humanity
with the fear that still produces manipulation,
ignorance, what was and will be
the art of the lie
with the aftermath of injustice
stalking the peoples through the centuries,
with the worst horsemen of the corniest Apocalypse.

Table of contents.

"*Resfalgio.*" (Subject): Children's narrative in poetic prose about the life of a cat in prison.
"*Three poets and a painter.*" (Theme): Brief poetic anthology of three Cuban poets, Pozo, Gerardo, Juan David, and a sample of drawings by painter Felix Villar.
"*In nostros*" (Theme): Allegorical poem. The poet, with dark and defiant touches, goes into places where the human mind has barely been able to delve. I have publishes this unfinished work.
"*Poetic Explosion*" (Theme) Poetry.
"*The edges of the wall.*" (Theme): Cuban social novel.
"*24 and a half hours*" (Theme): Novel of a Cuban exile, of an unfortunate or lucky cab driver in the city of Las Vegas.
"*The Secret Book of Luan Vidad.*" (Theme): What overflows thinking with truth and not gloom.
"*Poems that say something or nothing and other verses.*" (Theme) Poetry.
"*Remoteness*" (Theme) Poembook.
"*The keys of the earth.*" (Subject) Novel.
"*Of fireflies and solitudes.*" (Subject) Poetry.
"*The Two and the Cross.*" Novel covering the times of Emperor Tiberius and dealing with the two characters who were condemned at the side of the Messiah.
"*Cursed Poems.*" Poetry.
"*Of Love and Hate.*" Poems.
"*N*" (Theme) Science fiction novel.
"*The Alfredillo.*" Poetic prose and verses for my son Alfredo.
"*Intent Infinite*" (Theme) Poetry.
"*Talking to the Silence.*" (Theme) Narrative, political, social, cultural, and spiritual.
"*Notes from the last diary.*" Novel.
"*Love poems and soulless verses.*" Poetry.